The
TEN PRINCIPLES
from
EL CANTARE

VOLUME II

IRH PRESS

BOOKS
IRH PRESS
New York

ISBN 13: 978-1-942125-86-0
ISBN 10: 1-942125-86-0

Printed in Canada

First Edition

The
TEN PRINCIPLES
from
EL CANTARE

VOLUME II

RYUHO OKAWA'S FIRST LECTURES
ON HIS WISH TO SAVE THE WORLD

RYUHO OKAWA

IRH PRESS

Contents

CHAPTER ONE

The Principle of Wisdom

CHAPTER TWO
The Principle of Utopia

CHAPTER THREE
The Principle of Salvation

CHAPTER FOUR
The Principle of Self-Reflection

CHAPTER FIVE

The Principle of Prayer

Preface to the newly revised second volume of
The Ten Principles from El Cantare

There is a song, "How Far I've Come," and this song title expresses how I truly feel now. In 1988, Happy Science entered its second year since starting its activities, and I gave five public lectures that year. As the sequel to the five principles included in Volume I, this book contains the remaining five principles of the series. I, the author, at the time of conducting these lectures was 31-32 years old. These 10 basic lectures given in the span of two years, in 1987 and 1988, solidified the framework of the Happy Science teachings. Owing to these lectures and a few dozen publications, I gained up to 10,000 passionate believers and created Happy Science's foundation for progress, in contrast to my initial plan to control the membership from growing too rapidly.

The following year, in 1989, I gave a public lecture to 8,500 people at Ryogoku Kokugikan Arena, and in 1990, I gave public lectures at Makuhari Messe to about 10,000–20,000 people.

The lectures in this book contain words with spiritual power—words that are youthful yet filled with my wish to save the world. For words spoken by a religious leader, these lectures are far too original and boundless.

Ryuho Okawa
Master & CEO of Happy Science Group
August 9, 2020

Preface to The Principle of Enlightenment[*]

Attaining enlightenment is very hard. But remember that you can experience true happiness only when you have passed this severeness to attain enlightenment.

People are in fact very spiritual. When you leave this world, the only thing you can take with you to the other world is your mind. So enlightenment, which is the happiness of the mind, is all and everything. Don't think that you are happy when you have not developed spiritually or experienced a true awakening, for without these experiences, your happiness is only an illusion.

This book, *The Principle of Enlightenment*, which I preach to all people, is the eternal Truth that shall be passed on. This is the voice of the Eternal Buddha. Listen to this passionate and powerful speech.

Ryuho Okawa
Master & CEO of Happy Science Group
October 1990

Preface to The Principle of Utopia[†]

Energy and passion are necessary to save the world and its people. Come what may, we must overcome all difficulties and press forward on our path.

To create a true utopia, fighters that spread the Light of Truth must possess undaunted determination. Fighters who will create a path toward a bright future in this corrupt, clouded world, come and gather around me. A miraculous march is about to begin.

Unless the Light of Truth shines upon every corner of the world, humankind in the 21st century will have no future.

Now, we shall begin our indomitable march forward.

My strong wish to save the world—here it is.

My fellow fighters,

If you are warm-hearted human beings,

Listen to this true message.

Ryuho Okawa
Master & CEO of Happy Science Group
October 1990

[*] The title of the book published in 1990, containing Chapters 4 and 5 of Volume I "The Principle of Enlightenment" and "The Principle of Progress," and Chapter 1 of Volume II "The Principle of Wisdom."

[†] The title of the book published in 1990, containing Chapter 2 to 5 of Volume II "The Principle of Utopia" "The Principle of Salvation" "The Principle of Self-Reflection" and "The Principle of Prayer."

CHAPTER ONE

The Principle of
Wisdom

The First Public Lecture of 1988

Originally recorded in Japanese, on March 13, 1988
at Ota Ward Hall in Tokyo, Japan
and later translated into English.

1

The Basic Attitude toward Learning

A spiritual discipline suitable for people living today

Since establishing Happy Science, I have been not only exploring the Laws but also managing our group and the concerns of our staff, members, and readers. This position allows me to guide them as well as learn from them. During this time, I have contemplated the meaning of "wisdom"—the theme of today's lecture. We often use this word to describe the knowledge we gain from reading books or listening to others. Although "wisdom" is generally used interchangeably with "learning," differences lie in the content and purity of wisdom, scale of wisdom, and effects of wisdom. I have been pondering, speaking about, and writing about all these things. Today, I would like to focus on wisdom and speak about what I have been thinking about, writing about, and planning to write about it.

In the November 1987 edition of our monthly magazine, I wrote a short essay on the developmental stages of wisdom that briefly detailed how I have been confronting the theme of wisdom. In reality, I have been working on this theme for the past 10 years. Although I had never imagined giving this kind of talk in front of an audience, I have constantly felt an internal desire to improve myself. How can I sublimate this passion burning within me? This is the question I have contemplated for the past 10 years while thinking and acting within the world of ideas, the world of wisdom, and the world of experiences. Therefore, I would like to explain how I have thought about wisdom and how I have perceived wisdom based on my own experiences. This is important because my experiences over the last 10 years are reflected in and have been incorporated into our training contents at Happy Science.

I have repeatedly taught you that modern spiritual discipline is not attained simply by meditating in the mountains or obsessing over the desire for supernatural abilities. Then, what methods are there for the people of today, whether they are professional priests or lay believers, to walk the path of discipline? In finding this method, we need to consider the question about spiritual discipline and wisdom. In today's society, knowledge is highly valued in every walk of life. However, people tend to be concerned only with the superficial appearance and framework of knowledge without understanding its true nature, its essence, or what lies at its root. Through my experiences over the last 10 years, I have identified what lies deep within knowledge. This means there is a method of spiritual discipline that is safe and suitable for people living today.

This is what I mean by the method of spiritual discipline. If you merely explore and gain the knowledge that other people have already established and published, you will never discover the true blessing that knowledge can bring. But for those who have transcended this and have seen through to the great wisdom of humankind and to the very depths of the human mind and what lies there, great power can issue forth from knowledge. Those who have reached this wellspring of wisdom will experience infinite power welling up from within. The power of wisdom that gushes from the depths of this spring will serve as a great falchion sword that enables you to cut the Gordian knot and solve any difficulties in life.

In the past year, I have read hundreds and thousands of letters from various people (at the time of this lecture). My first impression was that many of these people do not properly understand the problems they are facing. They do not grasp the very problem they have and the exact nature of their problems. Next, they do not know how to solve them. What's more, they also do not know how to transform their problems into something better or higher that will lead them to happiness. Then, I realized the importance of having an intellectual foundation. This realization has led me to develop the current methods of training at Happy Science. So let me tell you how I established an intellectual foundation through my own experiences before delving deeper into the topic of wisdom as one aspect of the Laws.

Persistent attitude of "I will never think I understood something until I am fully convinced"

As mentioned in my short essay, I had a yearning for wisdom from a very early age. This yearning began during childhood but significantly intensified when I was 19 or 20 years old. My passion for learning welled up in waves from deep within me. During my youth, I was overwhelmingly passionate about learning and using my knowledge for a higher purpose. Unaware about my mission, my future work, or my destiny, I was swaying as to which path to take, but under these passions, I devoted all my energy every day to intellectually developing myself. Looking back to those years, many of the books I unconsciously chose to read contained the words and thoughts of angels (who were born on earth). I chose such books instinctively, like salmon swimming upstream as it follows a scent back to its birthplace.

In those times, one of the basic attitudes I considered necessary and important was, "I will never think I understood something until I am fully convinced." It is the attitude of never thinking I understood something until I am convinced of it in the deepest recesses of my mind. Until I grasp it completely, I will never stop studying or feel satisfied. I have been maintaining such an attitude. In due course, I explored many different fields of thought and study, including but not limited to literature, fine arts, science, philosophy, religion, poetry, business management, law, politics, economics, and international affairs. What is the great wisdom of humankind that continues to shine brightly like a diamond even today? I asked myself these questions over and over again.

I considered remaining in university and becoming a scholar multiple times, but one of the reasons I rejected this path was my mindset of not pursuing something unless I was fully convinced. Some among you may be educators at universities. The academic world today seems to have its own set of rules, and scholars conduct research only within the framework of these rules. Because the academic approach of Max Weber still dominates the mainstream modern research and the academic world, an analytical approach and objectivity are valued. Before presenting an original idea, one must investigate, quote, and document relevant ideas which others have already put forward. In such a restrictive world, many scholars think and read about various topics. To me, the existing academic system appears like the inside of a kaleidoscope—made of many tiny pieces of colored paper but displaying a very beautiful view. However, once you understand the true form of such a view, you realize that the "flowers" inside is not real. As I maintained the attitude of exploring everything to my heart's content and not acknowledging that I have understood something unless I have understood it thoroughly, most of the current academic fields were no longer a path for me.

Although I have been publishing many books of spiritual messages and other books on the Truth for some time, these contain very few background references quoted like, "As discussed by so and so" or "There are such and such thoughts." My books only reveal what I, myself, have pondered, practiced, and pondered again until I gained a complete understanding. My books of spiritual messages contain many unique teachings, but each of them struck a chord in my heart and radiated a bright light within me. In other words, they reflected my own thoughts. My policy is to never talk about or publish things I do not feel I have completely understood or I am not fully convinced of. I have explained in my first lecture, "The Principle of Happiness," that this is the starting point of Happy Science.

Now, in my lectures and books, I continue to hold to the policy of never revealing more than 10 percent of what I have learned. I believe I must hold back the other 90 percent to confirm that it is true. As such, the more books I publish and the more lectures I give, the more study and contemplation I need to do. I take this approach because only what we grasp through our hearts, not merely with our brains, ultimately becomes true nourishment for our souls. You have probably learned much at school or at work, but some knowledge you can and others you cannot take with you to the other world after death. The things you cannot take with you are the things you see and hear in life but pass and fade with time. When you finally leave this world, you can only take with you the knowledge that reached the very core of your soul and became a part of your character. Many people in society today live and work in the world of knowledge, but those who explore knowledge only within a world where words are mere symbols will soon realize that such knowledge is no more than a veil or a mask. Unless you grasp the true meaning that lies behind the words, you can neither gain true power nor take that knowledge with you to the other world.

This is not limited to Japanese writing; it applies to writings in all languages. Receiving education in English or learning foreign languages is now gaining popularity. When reading books written in other languages, I can clearly distinguish between those written in words that touch the very core of my heart and those that do not. A considerable amount of English is used in journalism, even when only considering the vocabulary; thus, completely understanding the content is difficult. Because sorting through and absorbing all the information that floods modern journalism is difficult, most of it will simply fade without a trace. There are, however, writings in simple English that touch the heart. For instance, the works by Oscar Wilde, whose simple words can easily be understood even by non-native English speakers, deeply touch my heart. What makes this possible? Because he uses plain English or Anglo-Saxon words that stand the test of time—words that have been part of the English language for centuries—his works inspire even non-native English readers.

I have published many books of spiritual messages, and I recommend that you read them. Because they are written in simple Japanese, they touch the hearts of many readers even though the contents are advanced. These books are written in words that have stood the test of time and are proven to have "spirit" dwelling in them. I can write in this manner because I have never deceived myself. I thoroughly explore everything until I am convinced I perfectly understand it, so I can express what I have understood in a simple way using "easy Japanese words."

Get rid of all vanity

Knowledge or wisdom is like embellishment or an accessory to those who have not deeply pursued it. It is just a collection of words. Bookstores are packed with uninspiring books written by authors interested only in the superficial meanings of words or the neat arrangement of words as symbols. These authors do not use the words that come from their souls—from the depths of their minds—or they have not discovered what lies deep within their minds. However, I only accept the knowledge I fully understand and have made this policy the foundation of my intellectual life. For this reason, I experienced the hardship of learning without a teacher. Now, you are learning through my lectures, but I was not able to do the same because I could rarely accept or completely agree with what other lecturers said. I was not easily convinced. Why was I not convinced? If the lecturer were following exactly the same direction as I was, our minds would resonate in harmony; otherwise, their world would unfold differently from mine.

The same goes for literature. From the perspective of Truth, even among famous masterpieces can be classified into high value and low value. However, most people cannot tell such differences. Some masterpieces are written by archangels (who are born on earth), whereas other works are written by writers attuned to the vibrations of hell. Nevertheless, the works of both are regarded as top-class. People are unaware of this. Nowadays, in general, literary works are evaluated merely based on the descriptions, the plot, and how the stories unfold. However, we must discover what lies beyond these superficialities. I have read many novels, and I suppose the authors reveal their own ideas, just as I am doing now in this lecture. They are therefore responsible for whether their work is worth reading, withstands the test of time, and enlightens others. If the authors do not thoroughly consider these points, then unfortunately, their work will only remain as material for recreational reading during teatime. When you read a book, you need to thoroughly seek what will be left after you strip or remove its superficial, embellished words and explore what the author truly wants to say.

This applies not only to literature but also to academic studies; you must remove all superficiality, embellishments, conventions, and rules to find the essence of academic studies. When you do this, no matter who the thinker is, you will find a condensed version of what the author is trying to say. The question is whether the core concept of a book is the Truth or not. When summarized in one page, does the book contain the Truth or not? What is the main message of the author? Regardless of how many books an author writes, if the core message is wrong, their works are of no value.

When exploring the world of wisdom, it is important to get rid of your embellishments and become "naked." We have workshops and seminars at Happy Science, and I have had the opportunity to read the essays written by members (at the time of this lecture). I often find that those in professions requiring intellectual ability write poor-quality essays; these people are generally concerned with their writing or showing off and are unable to reveal their original selves. I always ask members: What have you, yourself, grasped? What do you want to say? What have you truly understood? Please tell me. Please tell me in easy words that even children can understand. Unfortunately, not many people can. This means they have not gone sufficiently deep enough into their inner world or have not confronted themselves enough. If you wish to pursue wisdom, you need to reach this level; you must drop all pretenses and vanity to become your original self, grapple with the ideas of the authors head-on, and cultivate your own thoughts.

In the process of acquiring wisdom, you will meet many people, hear many arguments, and encounter many problems in life, all of which will challenge your philosophy to see if it is genuine or not. When met with such a challenge, if your thoughts are no more than embellishments or accessories, they will be blown away like dust in the wind. But if the thoughts you grasped are firmly rooted, they will be unshakable. Your thoughts will be refined as you accumulate various experiences, and this refinement will make your thoughts more and more brilliant. This is the attitude you should have toward wisdom.

Get rid of your vanity.

Remove your "accessories."

Become your original self.

Be pure in seeking wisdom.

If you explore knowledge merely out of a desire to look good in the eyes of others, it will lead you into a labyrinth.

You may come to believe you have become respectable or have attained enlightenment, but this is far from the truth. You can study for many hours a day and accumulate knowledge, but you need to examine whether you can explain what you have learned in plain language. This is the starting point.

You will know whether you have truly understood my books by examining if you can explain the contents in brief, simple words. If you cannot, you have not understood them. Only when you can speak at will on a theme—whether it is for five minutes, 10 minutes, one hour, or tens of hours more—can you say you have really understood what you have read. Merely quoting what is written on a certain page does not mean you have understood it. Please maintain this basic attitude.

If you continue reading with this understanding, who said what in which book will no longer matter to you. Only the essential wisdom that radiates light will remain in your soul, like the gold dust left in a sifting pan. You must sieve what you read and take the remaining gold dust. You must discover what you truly agree with at the bottom of your heart. This effort will create and develop the part of your soul that truly shines. I would like you to know that this is the basis of learning.

2

The Key to Unlocking Life's Problems

God gave us learning as a way to develop ourselves

Next, I would like to talk about the meaning of seeking wisdom. Why is it necessary to learn different things? Learning is closely related to the reason we have been given eternal life. We must first realize that learning is a path given to us by God. If learning were meaningless, then the fact that we repeatedly reincarnate over thousands, tens of thousands, or even millions of years would also be meaningless. The basic premise is that God values the act of learning.

So, what significance does God see in learning? We can find the answer in the discovery of our individual characters. A secret lies in the fact that each one of us is learning as unique individuals. Each individual is an artwork of God's Light and is brilliant like a rainbow arching over in the sky. A supreme being exists, who deems it wonderful to create this artistic diversity of light. It means each individual soul, with its own tendencies and personality, is expected to learn under the circumstances it is placed in.

Why are we required to learn so much? Why is learning considered so good? We need to consider this issue in the context of everyday life. Now, I would like you to ask yourself, "Why are you attending this lecture?" Can you come up with a clear answer? This is indeed important. Everyone is given problems to solve in his or her own unique circumstances based on the premise that you solve these problems on your own. People may give you advice, but in the end, no one except you can solve your problems. I doubt there is anyone who has no worries or problems. I bet you are all trying to solve your problems in some way and use them as a springboard to further improve your life. Perhaps you expect to find some clues in my lectures on how to solve your problems. Here lies the starting point of learning.

People are always looking for clues to better their life. We must solve our problems on our own, but the clues can be found all around us; both people who are living now and writers who have lived in the past can give us these clues. Therefore, we are learning to find the clues to help us solve our problems in life. This means God has given us a method to follow. He expects us to complete our unique workbook on our own but has also provided us with a reference book to consult. Moreover, we can meet our teachers of life or people who give us clues at the right time; this may happen at home or elsewhere. They are all our mentors or teachers at that given time. So finding clues to help solve our problems is the starting point of learning.

Insight is the key to solving your problems

What will happen once we have found the clues to help us solve our problems? What will be the result of collecting these clues? This is the next point we need to consider. If the varying opinions of different people only further confuse you, then the results will not be good. Your aim through learning is to attain greater insight. The secret to living a happy, productive, and noble life is having a high level of insight. Having greater insight means you have attained the key to solving various problems in your life.

As adults, we can easily find solutions to the problems children face. In contrast, it is difficult to help solve the problems of those in situations and positions similar to your own. Why? Because there is no difference between your level of insight and theirs. People who have a higher standpoint can easily solve the problems of those who have not yet reached that level; this is why people seek a teacher or mentor. Those regarded as teachers have a higher level of insight, so they can understand the causes of the other person's problem, find ways of solving it, and discern similar patterns the person might have experienced in the past. Those who understand the patterns can swiftly point out why someone has a problem and why they are unable to solve it.

However, if you are trapped in a whirlpool of suffering and your struggle seems like a matter of life and death, you would not be able to see why you have encountered such trouble no matter how hard you try. Let me explain using the example of a hen. Supposedly, hens are easily captive to their own imagination. When a hen who had been tied up with a rope is set free, the moment she sees anything long like a rope—even a line drawn with chalk—she will be unable to move because she thinks she has been tied up again. This illustrates how low the hen's *insight* is; because she has experienced being tied up in the past, seeing a rope can make her feel like she cannot move. We would pity such a hen; it all comes down to the difference between her level of insight and the insight of a human being.

A similar story from Algeria is about how to catch a monkey with a coconut. You carve a hole in the coconut that is just big enough for a monkey to stick its hand in, scoop out the flesh, put in some rice, and hang it from a tree. The monkey will stick its hand into the coconut and try to grab the rice inside. However, if it grabs the rice, it will not be able to pull out its closed fist. If it lets go of the rice, it can be free. But the monkey does not have sufficient *insight* to understand its own situation. The monkey knows it is trapped but has no idea of how to set itself free. Thus, on the following morning, it is easily captured. Despite desperately struggling to escape, it does not think to let go of the rice. This shows that the monkey does not have sufficient *insight* to reconcile its two desires—the desire for rice and the desire to be free.

Imagine yourself in the same situation. If you put your hand through a hole in coconut to grab some rice and could not take out your fist, you would immediately understand that you are stuck because your fist is bigger than the hole. You would instantly know that you can be free by letting go of the rice. Because the monkey does not have such *insight*, it falls into a deadly trap. This is a tragedy for the monkey. The monkey just wanted food and tried to take it but ended up falling into a life-threatening trap. Unable to escape, it suffers in agony until dawn. This is how we who live in this world appear through the eyes of the high spirits in heaven. We often suffer over trivial matters, just like this poor monkey, and struggle to see what the high spirits can see so easily. Nevertheless, for those who are desperate, this is a big problem, and we become completely clueless as to what we should do. This is what we fail to realize.

I like the writings of a French philosopher, Alain. Through his book, *On Happiness*, I discovered he was aware of some important truths. Let me give you a few examples from his book.

A baby keeps crying loudly, and no one knows what to do. The baby's parents wonder what is wrong. They wonder whether he wants milk or is too cold or too hot. In this way, the parents start to worry he might be sick and eventually call a doctor. The doctor finds nothing wrong with the baby, and the parents wonder further, "Why is my baby crying so loudly and so pitifully?" The cause of the problem turns out to be very simple—an open safety pin in the baby's garment. The baby was crying because the pin was pricking him. However, the adults were oblivious and were worrying a great deal, imagining many different possible causes. This kind of misunderstanding happens often.

There is another similar story. In the ancient kingdom of Macedonia, Greece, was an unruly horse that no one could ride. People had difficulty handling it and were looking for someone brave enough to tame it. Although this was considered a difficult challenge, one man succeeded quite easily. He alone understood that the horse was violent because it was afraid of its own shadow. He pulled the reins tightly so that the horse could not see its own shadow and calmed the horse down. The others could not understand the real cause, so they assumed the horse was violent by nature and was impossible to control with physical force. The horse had a habit of looking down and was frightened by its own shadow; it could not understand what a shadow was. The more furiously the horse struggled, the more energetically its shadow danced, creating strange patterns that terrified it. The solution to this problem was not to remove the shadow but to simply pull the reins tightly to keep the horse from looking down. Alain wrote such things.

After all, most difficulties in life end up becoming major problems owing to the lack of insight or the lack of ability to see the fundamental cause of the problem. The Truth is often very simple; it could be as simple as a pin in a garment or the fear of shadows. The causes of seemingly serious difficulties, including problems involving finance or business or problems of health or family, may also be very simple. We could be exaggerating the problems because of our ignorance. First, we must find the "pin" or the "shadow" in our problem. To this end, we need to take a step back and view our problems from a higher perspective. Then, we will discover an unexpected blind spot. Gaining greater insight is essential to see through these blind spots. This is "learning."

Your level of insight is your spiritual level

Those who have learned much in past incarnations have a higher level of insight. In fact, a person's level of insight is equivalent to his or her spiritual level. If I were to explain what a person's spiritual level means in this earthly world, it would be his or her level of insight—the question is whether he or she understands the feelings and worries of a greater number of people and to solve their problems. No matter how many books you read, without having greater insight, you will not attain the ability to solve problems.

People who have collected and assimilated clues to help solve life's problems and have established their own thoughts and ideas can instantly detect the worries of others and help solve them. The essence of learning is to acquire a higher level of insight. You need to acquire the ability to instantly understand that a baby is crying because a safety pin is pricking him—that is all. He is not asking for milk; he is not sick. A horse is not violent by nature but is simply afraid of its own shadow. However, people mistakenly believe it is an unruly, violent horse.

As we confront our own problems in life, we must never ever stop making a constant effort to acquire greater insight. That is why we need to study a wide variety of subjects. I publish many books, and one of the reasons for doing this is to provide you with as much material as possible to raise your level of insight. By reading the high-level thoughts of great men and women, sometimes you can easily find solutions to your problems. That is why I continue to publish many guidebooks to assist you in solving the problems you face in life. In seeking wisdom, acquiring and raising the level of our insight is most important. This is our spiritual training in this world. We need to use all that happens and all our knowledge to raise our level of insight.

The true nature of high spirits can be simply described as their high levels of insight. I teach that the spirit world is composed of different stages or dimensions: the fourth, fifth, sixth, seventh, eighth, and ninth dimensions. The difference between these dimensions lies not in the status or reputation of the spirits but in their levels of insight. The greater the position at which a person stands, the more worlds they have seen, the more people they have understood, and most importantly, the more they have grasped the Will of God. We are born into this world many times and accumulate experiences to gain greater insight.

When you face difficult problems or situations, the wisest approach is to discover a new source of insight. You need to try to clearly understand your own tendencies— that is, to understand the way you think about particular situations. For problems that repeatedly appear, try to find a solution more quickly. If a problem initially took you a week to solve, try to solve it in a day, an hour, a minute, or even a second the next time occurs. Such effort is, in fact, the driving force behind the development of human culture. Culture is created through the accumulation of such efforts.

If you need to start from scratch every time you are born into this world, there would be no base for culture to be built upon. We must take what our predecessors left us and build on top of it to move forward. Culture can be described as an accumulation of human insight.

Now, let me repeat the two main points I have made so far. First, as the basic attitude toward learning, never deceive yourself. Be honest, be true to yourself, and continue to explore until you become truly convinced of an idea. Second, the essence of learning is to acquire a higher level of insight. From this perspective, you will be able to understand the significance of your life in this world. When faced with life's difficulties, you must not be discouraged or worn out; instead, you must continually learn new lessons from your problems so that you can instantly identify the "pin" or the "shadow" and therefore raise your insight and gain a new perspective, even if it is by one or two levels.

3

The Developmental Stages of Wisdom

Having explained the importance of these two basic attitudes, I would now like to talk about the development of wisdom. The developmental stages of wisdom have never been explained in this manner. In my lecture in May 1987 ("The Principle of Love"), I explained that there are developmental stages of love. The same can be said of wisdom. Those who have already advanced to higher stages of wisdom can easily understand that there are different stages, but those who have not reached these stages cannot easily understand this.

1) "Continuing to seek for something higher" and "learning as an end"

To reach the first stage of wisdom, you must collect material to base your thoughts on. As I just mentioned, this is the way to acquire greater insight. To do this, having the attitude to learn many things, including the thoughts of those who are more advanced than yourself, is of utmost importance. This struggle to attain as much knowledge as possible is essential to reach the first stage.

Those who avoid this stage will only blindly accept the opinions of others. They end up being at a loss as to what to do every time they encounter a problem. However, those who aim to establish wisdom in this first stage can use what they have learned from their knowledge and experiences to increase the level of their insight. Because of this, they can quite easily solve most of the usual problems in life— problems that worry ordinary people for years. Thus, the benefits that accrue even at this stage are considerable. In the business world, too, many executives make considerable efforts to reach this first stage of wisdom. Top executives can instantly find solutions to the problems their subordinates struggle with and find impossible to solve. This ability can sometimes be described simply as "inspiration," but the intellectual effort is required before you start receiving such inspiration. The intellectual struggle within oneself is the attitude of continuing to learn, absorbing higher knowledge, and gaining enough confidence to feel you have assimilated sufficient knowledge. This self-confidence is essential in reaching the first stage of wisdom.

From a religious standpoint, this first stage of wisdom leads to the realization that the spiritual world really exists. I myself experienced this. By studying the works of various thinkers and further deepening that knowledge in my own mind, I began to more readily receive inspiration. Now, I have opened my spiritual channel, but this did not happen suddenly. Before this, there was a period when I received a lot of inspiration. I can think of two main reasons for this. First was that I constantly pursued something higher and continued to hold on to this attitude. The rule "Ask and you shall be given" applies in all situations; it also holds true for receiving spiritual inspiration. If you continuously seek for greater insight, a higher level of enlightenment, and a higher level of judgment, this attitude of constant seeking will invite the response of an outside power or other-power.

The second was the purity of my soul. As I mentioned earlier, you must get rid of your vanity. I assume many of you studied as a means to get into a better school, get a better job, or get a promotion. If you seek knowledge simply as a means to an end, you will not be able to pass beyond this first stage of wisdom. Why? Because this attitude casts a shadow on the purity of your soul. The essence that lies behind the academic study is the effort humans make toward gaining infinite wisdom. Unless you discover this truth, and if you pursue knowledge only as a means of achieving some worldly end, you will never go beyond the first stage. So you must understand the true meaning of "learning as an end" or "knowledge as an end." When learning is not a means but an end, when you find the joy of life in pursuing knowledge, and when you feel your soul being refined through this, you will reach the goal of the first stage of wisdom.

This is also the first stage of enlightenment. You will gradually receive inspiration and have peak experiences, or feel extreme happiness, quite often. Among the hundreds of books you read, you may come across one or two that are very impressive and touch you or move you to tears. Perhaps you have heard an inspiring talk and were so moved you could not stop crying. Such instances lead you to experience peak experiences or delights of the soul. This is actually the first stage of wisdom.

At this stage, you will feel as if a veil before your eyes has been lifted, allowing you to see the state of the world without the veil. Before this, you may have thought that people are trying to harm you or obstruct your path or that things often do not go as you wish, but once such ideas dissolve, you will discover that the world is truly wonderful. Helen Keller wrote of this truth in her autobiography. Despite her blindness, she had a wonderful view of the world and revealed that, to her, the world was a beautiful place.

Let me give you an example from literature. *A Christmas Carol* by Charles Dickens illustrates a similar transformation. This is quite a brief tale, so many of you have probably read it. The main character, Scrooge, is a mean old man whose only concern is making money. On Christmas Eve, Scrooge meets three ghosts—the ghost of the past, the ghost of the present, and the ghost of the future. Each ghost shows Scrooge scenes from his own life—how he was, how he is, and how he will be. First, the ghost of the past shows him how many people have suffered because of the way he has lived, constantly in the pursuit of making money. Then, the ghost of the present shows him the poor people who are suffering even on Christmas Eve. Finally, the ghost of the future shows him how he will die as a miserable and unloved person. After witnessing these scenes, Scrooge begins to repent deeply. He reflects on himself and realizes how wrong he has been living, how many people he has hurt, and how ignorant he has been of other people's pain. Then, at daybreak, a completely different world unfolds before his eyes. He has a truly wonderful Christmas Day. Everyone seems remarkable. Scrooge, who had always lived with a bitter expression on his face, now has a bright smile. To his surprise, people greet him with smiles, too. He discovers a new worldview. He realizes that the same world that appeared ugly before now appears beautiful simply because his mindset changed. Dickens created this story with exquisite skill, but from a religious perspective, this is one form of enlightenment. Those who have passed through the first stage of wisdom see this world as a truly wonderful place.

However, enlightenment at this stage is still rather fragile. In an isolated and tranquil environment where there is no cause for concern, you can probably maintain a peaceful mind free of worries; but you can still fall from this state. This state corresponds to the Arhat level of enlightenment we teach; at this level, the soul can still fall, just like how iron can rust without proper care. In other words, even the feeling of renewal that we all can experience at the moment of conversion or at the turning point to start a new religious life does not last for long. It tends to become forgotten in our daily routines. You need to figure out how to overcome this fragility and how to maintain a sense of freshness and a completely new view of the world. This is the big step toward the second stage of wisdom.

Once you have passed the first stage of wisdom, your level of insight will increase, and finding faults with others will be easy. You will be able to understand their problems, their concerns, and their weaknesses very clearly. However, even at this stage, your understanding will not be elevated enough to a love that sees their shortcomings from a higher perspective and embraces those people. It means you have not yet established unshakable wisdom. This is why you lose yourself in daily life or lack compassion and empathy toward others.

2) Building up unshakable confidence in your wisdom

Then, what kind of efforts are required to reach the second stage of wisdom? One requirement is to keep making steady, diligent efforts to study and learn. You must constantly make sincere efforts to accumulate knowledge without giving yourself any time limits. This attitude brings to mind the image of conifers and evergreens that never lose their green color even in winter. The leaves of many other trees turn red or yellow and eventually fall, but the leaves of pines and cypress remain green even in snow. We know from experience that these trees do not stand out in the summer, but they stay green and stand out in the winter. It is important for you to stand your ground like these conifers, even if circumstances change with the passing of time.

Can you remain fresh and evergreen even as others shed their leaves during winter? That determines victory or defeat. When you have an important exam approaching, or you are anticipating a promotion, you will probably have the motivation to work hard. When these "carrots" or opportunities to succeed are dangling before you, you can gallop like a horse, but the challenge is whether you can sustain that motivation when the carrots are taken away. The longer you can maintain your enthusiasm, the closer you will be to a historical great. Observing the lives of great historical figures, I am most impressed by their strong resolve and the spirit of perseverance. Regardless of the difficulties they faced or the suffering they endured, they always made an effort to overcome every hardship and never gave up. They constantly made efforts to maintain their greenery in the snow; through these efforts, their souls shone brighter. Experiencing difficult times is essential for strengthening the soul in the truest sense.

There are many ways to assess someone's true nature, but the best way is to observe the person on two occasions—in times of triumph and in times of great failure. Under these two circumstances, a person's true nature will be revealed. Some people become weak in times of triumph. As they are about to be in the limelight or the moment they are recognized, they quickly become satisfied and proud. These are the people who will not achieve great success. In contrast, some people give in to despair when faced with failure and only complain. They will not achieve success either. In times of despair, how long are you able to withstand hardship? During that time, can you calmly continue to strengthen your skills and refine yourself? The amount of perseverance is a measure of your true capacity.

When your status suddenly improves, how will you react? The one who soon grows proud cannot be regarded as a great person. The higher your position, the humbler you must become, and the more you must aim to make greater efforts. If you maintain this attitude, you will surely achieve great success. Note that one's true nature is revealed in these two extreme sets of circumstances.

To sum up, the second stage of wisdom is a period of endurance and of steadily building true self-confidence. The key during this period is to build self-confidence, accumulate experiences of success, and broaden your perspective. If you fail to build unshakable confidence in your own wisdom while you are at the stage of establishing yourself, you will eventually become jealous of others. You will feel insecure and jealous when you see someone on the same level as you, someone who seems more competent than yourself, or someone who achieves something remarkable. Experiencing this jealousy means you have not yet reached the second stage of wisdom. If you are truly absorbed in endlessly improving yourself, your mind will not be swayed by the successes or failures of others. Some people feel happy when others fail, and some people experience pangs of jealousy when they see others succeed. These people have not yet built unshakable confidence in their own wisdom. I have used the word "wisdom" here, but "enlightenment" or "insight" can also be used. These people have not yet firmly established the right way to see others, the world, and themselves.

At this stage, you will be tested to see how large your goal is and how diligent you are in accomplishing it. This test can last a long time, and many are unable to pass this stage in a single lifetime. Even if you are an exceptional person, whether you have an overwhelming love for others depends on whether you have moved beyond this stage. If you build unshakable confidence in your own wisdom, you will be free of jealousy and will be able to radiate a gentle light. The first stage of wisdom is a period of self-discipline, so there may be times when you show off your wisdom. However, when you reach the second stage—a period of being unshakable—you are taking a step toward becoming a great source of love to others.

3) The wisdom of service

Most people do not usually go beyond the second stage of wisdom, but I must admit there are even higher stages of wisdom. In the first and second stages, the development of wisdom is confined to the individual. In the third stage, however, wisdom transcends the individual level. This means a person's wisdom is no longer used for purposes of solving personal, everyday problems, such as resolving your concerns, giving advice to those around you, creating peace of mind, or finding a sense of happiness. At this stage, wisdom serves a higher purpose. This wisdom is not simply a collection of information or skills but is the knowledge that is transformed into love. As knowledge transforms into love, it becomes established as wisdom to be shared with many. This is when wisdom becomes its own philosophy.

Thinkers who present original ideas to the world through their writings or lectures are often at the third stage of wisdom. To write books that truly move people or to leave a lasting influence on future generations, the author must attain the third stage of wisdom. Here, wisdom transcends the individual level and is shared with many to inspire and encourage the spiritual progress of their souls. Wisdom at this level also becomes something of extraordinary volume. This is when a person's insight is no longer a personal asset but transforms into great wisdom for humankind.

This transformation requires many spiritual or mystical experiences, either of your own or through an encounter with someone who has had such experiences. Or it could also be a spiritual experience where you hit rock bottom but discover your divine nature after looking deeply into yourself. Leading an ordinary life will not take you to this third stage. Just before attaining this stage, people begin to see the possibility of using what they have repeatedly contemplated to benefit and guide others. This is when the knowledge you gain as an individual transforms into a love that serves others. This corresponds to advancing from the Light Realm of the sixth dimension, a world of intellectual pursuit, to the Bodhisattva Realm of the seventh dimension in the spirit world, a world of love. Only when you explore wisdom with the strong desire to be of service to many and actually translate this into action can you say your wisdom has reached the bodhisattva level. The wisdom that has not yet reached this level is of a lower stage than this.

This level of wisdom is most needed today. Although many people live an intellectual lifestyle, they merely enjoy that lifestyle within an individual framework. However, you should aim to reach the third stage of wisdom, the state of bodhisattva, where wisdom produces a harvest that can be turned into investments and more fruits in the future. You must not be satisfied with growing and enjoying the fruits of your own efforts. You need to aim to become a person who provides fruits to as many people as possible. I truly wish that all who listen to my lecture today attain the bodhisattva level of wisdom. Make a continuous effort and explore ways to translate and convey to others the wisdom you have attained to encourage them, inspire their souls, and illuminate their lives. I would like you to make this your aim.

4) Fundamental thoughts in human history

There is, of course, an even higher stage of wisdom—the wisdom of tathagata—wherein a person not only knows the secrets of living a successful life but also explores the treasures of humanity. In this fourth stage, wisdom becomes fundamental thoughts; for example, the wisdom of Socrates, Plato, and Aristotle in Greece, Confucius in China, Jesus Christ in Israel, or Shakyamuni Buddha in India. By introducing sources of thought, these great figures influenced the trends of not only people but also eras, cultures, and entire civilizations. They attained such great wisdom partly through numerous incarnations and continuous efforts; however, they also reached the level of fundamental thoughts that exist beyond the wisdom of bodhisattva that embraces love. This is the fundamental nature of guiding spirits viewed from the perspective of wisdom.

Many angels are born into this world to do more than just start religions. They teach the Truth to change the era and civilization, to create a new history of humankind, and to create a new people and new humankind. I, myself, continue to make efforts to firmly establish my teachings, condense them into wisdom, and translate them into universal love that transcends this age so that my teachings may be left for future generations. I hope that you, too, will explore the developmental stages of wisdom through the guidelines I have outlined and aim toward this goal.

CHAPTER TWO

The Principle of Utopia

The Second Public Lecture of 1988

Originally recorded in Japanese on May 29, 1988
at Osaka International House in Osaka, Japan
and later translated into English.

1

Facing the Age of Crisis

Today, four of my books were released for sale. I believe the one that drew the most attention was *The New Prophecies by Nostradamus* (which includes spiritual messages from Nostradamus, John the Revelator, and Elijah). It contains unreleased content that was recorded a few years ago. But why did we publish this book at this particular time? We have been emphasizing the importance of individual effort and teaching that destiny can be overwritten by one's efforts. Then, why are we publishing such prophecies? During the process of publishing these prophecies, I faced many internal conflicts. I anticipated the impact of the prophecies on people and the responsibility that comes with making such prophecies public. Am I ready to be held accountable? I had to ask myself this question.

I started receiving spiritual guidance from the heavenly world seven years ago (at the time of this lecture). As I have repeatedly shared with you, I always assess my achievements. I only build upon the things that I am certain about, using them as the foundation for the next step. This has been my method for making progress; this is how prudent I have been as I tread this path. Although I have received many spiritual messages, if they do not truly have the power to enrich this world and make people better, I do not make them public. This has been my stance all along. However, at times, one must say what must be said.

Let me take you back 2,600 or 2,700 years, when Israel had many prophets. Among them was Hananiah, who is now known as a false prophet. He gained popularity by denying the prophecies that foretold any terrible events and proclaimed that only good would manifest in this world. With his optimistic messages, he won the trust of common people and the people in high positions. Hananiah was reborn in Japan in recent times and founded a certain religious group. He passed away almost seven years ago.

Now, let me tell you the truth. Is it right to turn a blind eye to the evil in front of you and stay silent? If the age of crisis is coming, we must sound the alarm to let people know what is upon them and help them prepare for it. This is one way of thinking. After wavering over the decision to publish the prophecies, I decided to publish them because the crisis of humankind is approaching. Nostradamus, John the Revelator, and Elijah foretold the arrival of the age of crisis. Not all of their prophecies coincide with each other; this is clear when you read *The New Prophecies by Nostradamus*. However, the baseline of their warnings is the same.

Such prophecies have been made not only by those who specialize in predicting the future but also by Buddhist and Christian spirits in different spiritual messages. When preaching the teachings of the mind, they also explained how to be prepared for difficult times. Although the Buddhist monk Hui-kuo cautioned against revealing predictions of a dark future, he implied dark times were approaching. Similarly, the Japanese Christian leader Kanzo Uchimura, who was cautious about not saying anything negative, predicted the arrival of the age of crisis.

What if such a dark age is about to be realized? What if the prophecies were to come true according to the timeline revealed to us? What if this movement of Happy Science is indeed what Nostradamus foretold as the "Opposite of the Darkness" that creates the future beyond the year 2000? Then, we must gather our forces to take action and create a movement to counter the darkness.

There is little time left to avoid the age of crisis. According to the prophecies, the crises of humanity will manifest in some form within the next 10–20 years. If the prophecies come true, what must be done? What will you do? What will I do? This must now be considered. You may be busy working at a company every day, but if the prophecies were to come true sometime during the 1990s, what will you do? One of the prophecies says that a catastrophic event will occur in one of the cities in Japan. (Note: The prophecy might have been about the Great Hanshin-Awaji Earthquake [January 17, 1995] or the Great East Japan Earthquake [March 11, 2011].) Such an event could trigger the beginning of the age of crisis in the country and beyond. When disasters become a worldwide phenomenon, what will you do? What will you seek? Where will you go? How will you take action? This is not just about you but also about other people. What would happen to those who did not anticipate any disaster? Whom should they rely on, and where should they go? If people cannot see the light toward the future, they will surely panic in the darkness.

Consequently, we are in a dilemma. On one hand is our objective of solidifying the foundation of our organization and spending time on each and every person who has gathered, helping them reveal and refine their Buddha-nature or divine nature. On the other is the great urgency to begin our missionary work. So what are we to do? To solve this dilemma, it won't be enough to inform people of the approaching crisis and let them develop a sense of crisis. To cancel out the darkness, we must bring the opposite of darkness. To remove people's fears, we must offer hope.

2

The Three Guiding Principles to Realize Utopia

Then, what is the principle of hope? What is the "Principle of Utopia" as we head into the worst times? Now, I would like to discuss the subject of utopia, an idea that will completely disappear from people's minds for some time. We are now in a transition period, where we need to overcome difficulties and steadfastly prepare to usher in a new age.

There are three main guiding principles that constitute the "Principle of Utopia."

The first principle—establishing the age of spirituality

The first one is to establish the age of spirituality at this time because there will be no other time. Various crises may occur, but we must not simply dismiss them as crises and make escaping them our only goal. We must be wise enough to recognize that this is staged. Because we live in such times, we can use crises to our advantage and make great strides toward establishing a spiritual age. Using every opportunity to move forward in a better direction and to lay the foundation for the future is important.

In Japan, for example, what portion of the population believes in the existence of the other world, the spiritual world, or believes that the soul is the essence of a human being? Perhaps about 20 percent. Among this 20 percent, how many are convinced? How is the Truth, which has existed for more than hundreds of millions of years and was earlier accepted as a matter of course, not accepted by people in these advanced times? How can we live each day without knowing the Truth? What kind of people are we? What is the basis for our existence? As we ask ourselves these questions, I have to admit that our present-day civilization is founded on complete delusions.

I have been revealing messages from high spirits in heaven who are endeavoring in many ways to provide proof of the existence of the Real World. Their conclusion is one. The other world exists because it does; it exists because it is actually there. Just as countries like Japan and the United States exist, the other world also exists; the high spirits are making this clear. The existence of the Real World should not be doubted based on whether people can see it or accept it. In the Real World, or the place we return to after death, the rule of reincarnation is easier to understand than first-grade math. It is common knowledge. Yet this simple rule is beyond the understanding of the so-called intellectual elites of the present age. What, then, is the nature of the knowledge possessed by these intellectuals? What kind of knowledge do they gain? What do their studies consist of? Their knowledge amounts to nothing more than a collection of worthless and unnecessary information. In this way, the time has come to deny all things that are considered valuable.

God sometimes takes drastic measures beyond our imagination. I believe this is because God's love contains not only the obvious care and kindness but also another, higher level of love that has the decisiveness to perform "surgery." God will perform "surgery" in times when it will otherwise be too late to save humans. As the time for surgery draws near, my anxiousness increases, similar to a worried family member. I hope everything will go smoothly, but I cannot help but worry about the outcome. Will the surgery be successful? The massive chaos that is to come is not limited to this world; it will also happen in the spiritual world. Many people will leave this world: this is already mostly determined. How will we settle the chaos in the spiritual world when hundreds of millions of people suddenly return there? It will be a difficult challenge.

The fact that we were born in these times undoubtedly indicates we are living in the climax of the play or scenario directed by God. Given the terrors of this climax, you are given a choice to leave or to stay until the end. The more I think about it, the more I realize the endless nature of our mission. The scope of our work that lies ahead—the number of people the Truth must reach and the breadth and depth of the teachings that must be taught—is vast and limitless. However, the Truth must spread to every corner of Japan at least within the next three years. (Note: Starting with the Celebration of Lord El Cantare's Descent on July 15, 1991, a total of 10 lectures were held in Tokyo Dome over five years, and the lecture in 2017 was broadcast to 3,500 locations around the world.) We are currently planning how to go about attaining this goal.

The second principle—reforming economic principles

I have explained the necessity of thoroughly establishing the age of spirituality at the beginning of a new era as the first principle. The second principle is to reform economic principles. Over the last few hundred years, capitalist principles have spread all over the world. And businesses work based on these principles. This is now accepted as common sense. However, is capitalism really common sense? I dare say, "No."

In March, I published *Shin Business Kakumei* (literally, "The New Business Revolution") that introduces my theory of new economic principles. To put it bluntly, the way we do business now is wrong. Why do 70–80 percent of people, or perhaps more than that, work to make a livelihood believing that the pursuit of profit is the highest ideal or principle? Have you ever questioned this idea? I am not saying seeking profit is wrong; I am saying people must be clear about their reason for pursuing profit. If you work for a company, you know how important profits are. But please ask yourself, "For what purpose?"

In fact, this philosophy of chasing profit is the contemporary form of bad religion. You need to understand how poisonous it is for your soul to have such a creed implanted in you. The profits of economic activity are acceptable only when they are used for some purpose. What purpose is that? As a negative condition, profits must not be used to corrupt people. (Note: A few years later, in 1990, an economic crisis occurred in Japan—the bubble economy burst.) As a positive condition, profits must contribute to the happiness of society. When these two requirements are ignored, the worship of materialism, which most people today are engaged in, turns into evil. You must realize that chasing profit is a type of idolatry—profit has become a kind of false idol. In other words, the Baal god is worshipped everywhere. This evil worship of materialism is prevailing, and we must break through this altered form of worship of materialism.

In truth, profits should correspond to the evaluation of people's activities. People engage in various activities or work, but how should we evaluate their work? One evaluation method is the monetary value system. However, this method is still very primitive and low level. In the Real World, too, an economic system based on money exists. For example, in the Astral Realm of the fourth dimension, the monetary currency is used. The currency is not made of matter, of course. People created it through their thoughts because they felt the need for it. The fifth dimensional world has an economy based on a kind of exchange system. The sense of economic activity only remains until the Light Realm of the sixth dimension, where values are measured not by the amount of money or goods a person receives but by the number of thoughts of gratitude. Therefore, this realm has an economy based on thoughts. In the world above that, the Light of God functions as an economic principle. The value of people's activity is clearly evaluated by the amount of light they are given from God. One indicator of this light is the halo or aura. Halos, in fact, represent God's currency. This is something you must know—the value or currency that is valid in the other world is the amount of Light of God. Those who have done a considerable amount of work will be evaluated accordingly, and the value can be manifested as an aura or light. In this sense, light is just like money in this world and therefore can be accumulated. Light is given according to the level and amount of good work done in accordance with God's Will. This is the economics of the world of Truth.

This economics does not only apply to the other world. To a certain extent, the same system also works in this earthly world. Perhaps you cannot directly see the amount of light you receive from God, but its effects manifest indirectly and in various ways. For instance, the light sometimes manifests as good health or as success at home or in business. At other times, this God-given "currency" may manifest as good character. So the economics of the kingdom of God also holds true in this world, although somewhat indirectly. Accordingly, two types of currencies are circulating in this world. One is the currency issued by the central bank and the government, and the other is issued by God. These are not completely separate; they are sometimes interchangeable. In certain markets, both are valid; however, in other instances, they are not interchangeable at all.

Our target is to establish a new economic system where these two currencies blend—where the two tides meet. The economic principles of the future must head toward a system in which the worldly values accord with the values of Truth, which reflect God's Will. This will help the economic principles in this world correspond to the other world. This is what I am advocating.

Ultimately, we are trying to dismiss what Jesus said 2,000 years ago—"Give to Caesar what is Caesar's and to

God what is God's." We are working to move past Jesus. He taught about realizing the kingdom of God. He said, "Repent, for the kingdom of heaven is at hand." Jesus was born to establish the kingdom of God in this world, but his "kingdom of God" could not expand beyond the "kingdom of the mind." However, the kingdom of God we are now trying to establish applies to both the inside and outside of our minds. We cannot accomplish our mission in this lifetime without transforming this earthly world into heaven.

The third principle—establishing and mastering major principles for action

To this end, the principles behind our actions can be classified into two types. One is the principle of repentance of the individual or personal enlightenment, and the other is the principle of repentance of the entire society or the reformation of society. These are two "swords"—one long and one short. We have appeared in this world with these two swords and are determined to bring about a global reformation with them. Without these two swords, we cannot change this age.

If our aim was to focus only on the kingdom of the mind, we would have no reason to begin missionary work in this present age or for me to dedicate myself to giving fervent lectures throughout the country. This has been done 2,000, 3,000, 10,000, and even 100,000 years ago. We cannot simply make the same effort each time we are born into this world; we must move forward to achieve higher goals. So, as the third principle, establishing and mastering the two major principles for action—reforming both the individual and the society as a whole—to create the kingdom of God is essential.

3

The Principle for Action to Create Utopia

< *To create a utopia in your mind* >

1) Build the desire to change yourself

Now, as the first step, by giving lectures and publishing books, I am primarily teaching you how to build the kingdom of the mind. In March 1987, at Ushigome Public Hall, I introduced the Principle of Happiness that consists of four elements: love, wisdom, self-reflection, and progress. This teaching is a modern version of Hinayana (Small Vehicle) Buddhism. Our teachings still weigh heavily on Hinayana (as of 1988; Happy Science later began leading a movement to save all people). The first stage of creating utopia begins with the principle of the mind or the teachings of the mind. This is a set rule.

Why is that so? Let me ask you this: If you claim that you can only be happy when your environment or conditions change, then why do you go through many reincarnations in many different eras and play different roles? Can you explain the reason for this? If you like being a king, you could have been born a king in every life. But no one chooses to be a king in every reincarnation; they become kings, then beggars, then middle-class citizens, and they take on different roles as they walk along their paths of life. The truth is that there is a basic law, an important guiding principle of the entire universe: "No matter your environment, establish the kingdom within you. Establish a utopia in your mind." This is an unspoken law that has remained unchanged throughout the long history of humankind.

How can you create an ideal world in your mind right now? What do you think are the principles for creating a utopia in your mind? What do you need to do to get closer to what Jesus called "the kingdom of God"? To create a utopia in your mind, you at least need to know about the lives and thoughts of the people who actually live in the kingdom of God. Without this knowledge, you cannot. Then, what reference material is available? I have been publishing many books of spiritual messages for this exact purpose. I am trying to inform people of the mindset they need in order to bring the kingdom of God into their minds. You must learn from great figures in history. I want people to know the mindsets of those who made it to heaven. That is why I am publishing spiritual messages of famous historical figures. Of course, you could also learn from bad examples. You could learn what not to do by exploring the ways of living that lead to hell or by learning from the outcomes of certain mistakes. However, first and foremost, I want to teach and show you a good example to use as a guide. That is why I have been publishing many books of spiritual messages one after the other.

Please look at the way the famous historical figures thought and lived. If you feel your mindset is on par with theirs, you have done well; please continue to live as you do now. However, unfortunately, I imagine the majority of you have not yet reached this level. If you were to die at this very moment and become a spiritual being, would you be able to say something similar to what the high spirits said? If you could, then you are on their level. What do you think? In my books, I present model cases for you to follow as the ideal ways of living.

What comes after studying these cases? Here is the next challenge. Turn your attention inward and ask yourself if you have the will to change yourself. This is the starting point and also the prerequisite for joining Happy Science. To become our member, you are required to practice the exploration of the Right Mind. Perhaps many people only understand it superficially and believe they are doing well. But I would like to ask them, "Are you really willing to change your own mind?" That is what I am asking for. At this moment, there are very few people who live according to the Will of God in this corrupt world we live in. Please accept this first. The exploration of the Right Mind requires you to change yourself. Are you willing to correct the way you think and behave as soon as you find your mistakes? If you are satisfied with yourself as you are now and cannot see any need to change or improve, then we are not on the same page.

Please do not think of the exploration of the Right Mind as an abstract idea; it is essentially your willingness and energy to change yourself. If you are not willing to change your mind, you can leave our group. Our teachings are not meant for those without the will to improve themselves. If you find that you have not yet established the kingdom of God in your own mind, make steadfast efforts to improve and innovate yourself. If you don't have this desire, you do not qualify as a Happy Science member. If you think you have already attained enlightenment, you can preach your own teachings as a founder, or you can continue to live in a completely different world. This may sound harsh, but I must first make it clear that those who are satisfied with the way they are now and are not willing to transform themselves do not qualify as our members.

After all, there is a tremendous gap between the state of mind of people living in this third dimension and that of spirits living in the Real World of the fourth dimension and beyond. Unless you are determined to change your own mind, the mind will not change. From the perspective of the high spirits in the Real World, this world seems uncertain and unstable, like walking on the ocean floor or through a mirage in a desert. That is why you must not be content to remain as you are now. Reevaluate your mind and change it. Motivate yourself and be determined to establish the kingdom of God within. This is the starting point.

In Buddhism, this is called *bodhicitta* or "the mind pursuing enlightenment." Shakyamuni Buddha emphasized its importance, too. People cannot change unless they aspire to do so. Will they change if you give them money? Maybe, for some time. But deep down, they will not change. How about if you build them a house? They might change temporarily. But their basic character will not change. To establish the kingdom within, changing your own mind is the only way. No one else can do this for you.

Within each one of you is the kingdom of the mind, and each one of you has been given the key to open it. There is no spare key. Unless you open it yourself, the door to the kingdom of your mind will not open. Everyone has a key. I have said this in many ways on many different occasions. Open your mind with the key you carry with you. It is as simple as that. I have been providing you with a lot of reference material, so you must awaken to this simple truth. All Happy Science members or members-to-be, please have strong determination. I would like you to have the strong will to change yourself. There is a tremendous gap between how God wishes you to be and how you are right now.

I feel the burning passion of the high spirits. They earnestly wish people to awaken to the kingdom of God. But no matter how passionately they try to communicate their messages, people regard these messages merely as words in books. They are not aware of just how much the high spirits are putting their very hearts and souls into their messages. Please put yourself in their place. Imagine you have left this world to become an angel in the other world. How would you feel about the way people are living today? What would you do? You would become deeply aware of how ardently the high spirits are watching over us; unfortunately, I cannot fully convey what I perceive. Nevertheless, I can at least say this: "You have the key. Take the key you have there with you. Put it into the keyhole and open the window of your mind." Unless each of you truly awakens to the kingdom of God, the energy to save people will never well up from within you.

Sometimes you might feel that God is unfair. You might ask yourself why there are such vast differences in people's living conditions, their environment, gifts and abilities, houses, parents, family background, income, physical strength, and so on. However, God treats us all equally in one aspect—God has given each one of us the key to open the door within.

2) *Accumulation and missionary activity of Truth*

I have just mentioned that you first need a strong will and energy to change yourself. Then, what about the second step? The second step has two parts. In the first part, you need to accumulate inner resources. In our current lives, we have spent almost all of what God has given to us. Before we are born, God gives each of us a certain amount of "funds" as a travel allowance. However, we forget the main purpose of our journey and use the funds on trivial matters along the way. Instead of using this precious gift for its intended purpose, we often spend it on other things. We must realize that unless we stop doing this, we will not reach our destination. Now, look back to your starting point and begin to accumulate internally. Start accumulating the energy of the Light of God, the knowledge of the Truth, and the energy of love. This is very important. You have already depleted your travel allowance and therefore must start saving again. This is one of the steps you need to take after having determined to change yourself.

For more than 40 years, Shakyamuni Buddha repeatedly taught the importance of cultivating internal resources and storing spiritual nourishment within. This storage becomes the source from which you are able to give to many others and enrich their minds. Of the different types of offerings, conveying the Truth is by far the greatest. Unless you have internally accumulated the Truth, you cannot teach it to others. That is why I emphasize the importance of knowing and studying the Truth. Do not mistake the order that should be followed: explore the Truth, learn it, and then convey it to others.

Let me individually explain each element. "The exploration of the Truth" means to take an interest in the Truth, gather knowledge and information with a questioning mind, and constantly store knowledge of the Truth for the future. "Learning the Truth" means assimilating the knowledge you have accumulated and honing it as a tool you can use whenever needed. Only collecting many teachings of the Truth is not enough; you need to be ready to make active use of them. In other words, do not be satisfied with just studying the books of Truth. Think about how you can assimilate what you have learned and use it in the next step of your development. Think about how to apply it. Establish your own way of doing this. Until then, you cannot say you have "learned" the Truth. This learning certainly does not mean simply accepting what is written without question or memorizing what you have read or heard. Your learning must go deeper. Ask yourself how you can apply the Truth to yourself and the people around you. From this perspective, reintegrate and reorganize the knowledge of the Truth within you. Only then can you say you have learned the Truth.

Next comes "conveying the Truth to others." We know that the second step of creating a utopia in the mind has two parts: the principle of inner accumulation and the principle of missionary activity—namely, conveying the Truth to others. After you have truly learned the knowledge you have accumulated, how are you going to present it to others? The more you learn, the more you can teach others. The more knowledgeable you are, the broader your range of activities will be.

Religions nowadays are poor in quality because they lack the principle of missionary work. They are often unable to present their teachings in ways that are appropriate for people's circumstances and mindsets. This is why many religious groups are seen as outsiders in society. They are just proud of their teachings and think all they have to do is relay the divine messages they received. That is why they are misunderstood and snubbed. This is where they are going wrong.

Of course, the Truth should be conveyed to others, but you must first assimilate it as your own. Once you have assimilated it, convey it in your own words. Digesting the Truth until it is incorporated into your very actions is important. Please study the teachings in my lectures and books to the point where you forget that you were ever studying them. Study them to the point that you feel they have always been part of you. Only then can you talk to others about the different teachings in your own natural and unique way. Regardless of who said it, if you heard something that resonated deep in your heart and touched your soul today, then make it your own. Transform it into your own philosophy. Make it your own personal creed. Once you have made it your creed, what will you do? How will you incorporate it into your daily life? How will you convey it to others? I am saying you must take action as a small part of the kingdom of God.

I repeatedly emphasize the importance of first learning the Truth before conveying it to others because this is where the mistake of the modern religious and spiritual world lies. They have not assimilated what they have learned. They have not managed to establish their own kingdom within. Nevertheless, they go to their neighbors and try to open the lock of their neighbors' minds using their own keys. This attitude is wrong. Each individual is responsible for opening the lock of his or her own mind. If you want to encourage others to unlock their minds, you must use your own key to open the window of your mind first, at the very least. I would like you to perceive the kingdom of God for yourself. I would like you to fully realize that this is the way God wishes you to live.

When you do this, you will feel harmony in your mind. You will experience great joy, a powerful emotion that moves you, and you will definitely feel that you have been reborn. If you have not experienced this feeling—the feeling of being born anew and becoming a different person—welling up from within, then your mind is yet to be unlocked. So delve deep into your inner self until you truly feel you have been reborn. Those who are completely satisfied with remaining at a shallow level are creating confusion in this world. I sincerely hope you will experience moments of incomparable bliss in this lifetime. I want to help you savor this bliss. I want you to know how wonderful this moment of happiness feels. I wish for as many people as possible to part from their false selves and experience the joy of discovering their true selves who have always been loved by God. This is one of my most important missions. Most people do not know this bliss. If they can experience it while they are alive, they will not be confused in the afterlife and will not suffer in the other world. People suffer because they put off seeking this bliss until after they return to the other world. But I would like them to experience it in this lifetime.

The emancipation Buddhism teaches does not mean you will return to a higher spiritual world and never be reborn into this world. What emancipation truly means is to cast off the heavy armor-like attachment you have to worldly things. I am telling you to take off your armor to reveal your diamond self. All of you are wearing heavy iron armor on your mind that rattles as you walk. From a spiritual perspective—in the eyes of the high spirits—you seem to look ridiculous. Take off your armor, now. If you were one of these high spirits, you would surely want to help people reduce their load. So cast off your armor. Experience lightness and how pleasant the feeling is. To experience this, first, generate the energy to change yourself; then, seriously learn the Truth and master it. Finally, apply it to your everyday life. This is essential.

Once you truly learn how much you have received from God, this understanding will lead to action. The knowledge that is not converted into action is not true knowledge. When you truly know, when you have truly learned, your body will move on its own; your feet will move, your hands will move, and your mouth will move. You will not be able to stay still. You will want to convey the Truth. That is what truly absorbing the Truth means. True "learning" is not one that simply goes in one ear and comes out the other. Your body will begin to move on its own. I would like you to experience this state of mind first.

3) Experience the true nature of the spiritual world

So far, I have discussed the first two steps of establishing the kingdom of the mind. The third step involves discovering the world you never knew about in this lifetime. I would like you to see and experience the true nature of the spiritual world—the Bodhisattva Realm and the Tathagata Realm—while you are still alive in a physical body. I want you to discover such a world by yourself and not just hear about it from others. This is very closely related to "opening the window of your mind" and can also be explained as "opening the spiritual channel." This is the next stage.

Because I am currently focusing on establishing a solid foundation of Happy Science, I have not been actively guiding you to open the window of your mind. However, many people will experience it when the time comes. (Note: As of March 2022, Happy Science has more than a dozen spiritual experts.) I predict that many of them will discover more than just their inner conscience or their guardian spirit. They will realize the existence of an infinite treasure house deep within themselves. I also predict that more and more people will discover the true nature of angels and the true nature of the Kingdom of Light. Only when people reach this state of mind will they have the power to act, the light to act, the energy to act, and the serious will to act.

As I said in my lecture "Development of the Mind" during the seminar in Gunma Prefecture in May 1988, we are not born into this world merely for those who came from heaven to return to heaven. Our work in this life is to nurture many angels in this world. When the world sinks into darkness, we need light. We need angels. If we cannot get enough angels from the Real World, we simply have to nurture them in this world. Yes, we will. We will nurture many angels in this world. And before that, we will nurture many fighters or people who will fight on God's behalf. This is very important. We cannot wait for high spirits to be reborn and start preaching the Laws. Unless people of great potential among you come forth, the salvation movement will not start in the truest sense. Do not wait for high spirits to be sent from heaven. You, yourself, must become one of them.

Become a bodhisattva in this lifetime. Become a tathagata in this lifetime.

You have to make efforts to get there. You have already been given sufficient resources to do so. If you are able to thoroughly study what you have been given and put it fully into practice, you will be able to attain the state of bodhisattva or even tathagata. You have already been given enough resources for that. Whether you reach this state is up to each and every one of you.

I would like you to become bodhisattvas. There is nothing wrong with having a thousand bodhisattvas or producing extraordinary tathagatas from among you. The world demands light, so why not come forth?

Come forth, bodhisattvas. Come forth, tathagatas.

I hope bodhisattvas and tathagatas will emerge from among you and those we meet in the future. Do not concern yourself with your past lives. A past life is a past life, and this life is this life. Separate yourself from your past and become a light in this lifetime. Make an effort to become a light in this life. Some might need hundreds, thousands, or tens of thousands of years to do so, but never mind that. In the world of Truth, the concept of average speed does not exist. The moment you think, you can change. This is the nature of the world of Truth. You must know that there is no time in the world of the mind. In the world of the mind, in the world of the soul, time does not really exist. The very moment you think, things change. This is the true state. It is the state that Zen Buddhists are ultimately trying to achieve.

Become a bodhisattva right now. Become a tathagata right now.

I am telling you so. Why not? You have all the necessary resources. Why not take up the challenge? Why not take action? You are living on Earth. You can convey the Truth to more than a hundred million people. All these people are waiting for you to take action. What are you waiting for? Wake up. Now, stand up.

Make sure you firmly grasp the three steps for building utopia within yourselves. Do not hesitate to become a bodhisattva or tathagata. If you feel you are not quite ready, then at least have the fortitude to become a fighter and fight to establish the kingdom of God. With these efforts, new angels will be born. Everyone can reach this level. Why not achieve it?

Why do you think I am publishing spiritual messages? Why are so many high spirits appearing here? Why is Jesus Christ sending us spiritual messages? Why is Moses? Please think about this. Isn't it because an event that occurs only once every several thousand years is happening? This is the reality before your very eyes. Jesus spoke, and his words are in my books. What does he expect of you? Please ask yourself these questions. Why is Nostradamus telling us to "create the 21st century and beyond"? Who is listening to these words? It is you, isn't it? So, if you don't create it, who will? The people of the future? The people of the past? The people outside of your country? Who exactly? Please ask yourselves.

The only goal of the principle of utopia on an individual level is to make angels. There is no other way. By making angels, this world will turn into Buddha Land. The greater their number, the greater their power to create an ideal world. Please never forget this idea.

< *To create utopia in society* >

So far, I have discussed the principle of creating a utopia in the mind. Next, we must establish the principle of creating utopia in society. What is this principle? It is to make the Truth spread throughout this three-dimensional world. In other words, it means to practice the teachings given by God and realize wonderful results as proof based on the laws of cause and effect.

Who will prove the authenticity of the teachings I preach or write about in my books? We need proof. Those who have read and understood the Truth must prove its authenticity by putting the laws of the mind into practice and actually changing society. For example, you learned that the new economic principles based on the Truth need to be established, but who will actually demonstrate what would happen in society when these principles are put into practice? You, yourselves, of course. You must put the Truth into practice in your workplace and your society. Then, you need to logically and scientifically, according to the law of cause and effect, explain what will happen if you do so. You must prove that society will be reformed and that this world will transform into Buddha Land by acting in accordance with God's Will.

Unless you prove it in this world and actually confirm it with your own eyes, you cannot say you truly accomplished anything. Do not only make subjective judgments. Do not get tricked into thinking your work is done. Do not be conceited. Confirm the changes that occur in reality. Experience for yourself that the changes really do occur, that society can be reformed, that the world can change, and that people's minds can change. Realize this. Acknowledge this. Confirm it. Prove it. This is how far you must go.

Furthermore, the inner change that occurs in you must become a truly great tide of love that has the power to change the minds of many. Otherwise, the change is not real. We must prove that what is truly valuable in this world cannot be seen with our eyes. For example, God, love, mercy, courage, and faith have true value and are truly meaningful and significant. We must let people know this fact and that we live in such a great river of love. The principle of utopia will truly be manifested only when this is achieved.

Everyone! In this society, where people only believe in what they can see, let us take action and launch a movement to let people know the value that lies in what cannot be seen. Let us all work together to accomplish this mission.

CHAPTER THREE

The Principle of Salvation

The Third Public Lecture of 1988

Originally recorded in Japanese on July 31, 1988
at Edogawa General Culture Center in Tokyo, Japan
and later translated into English.

1

Be Creative and
Make Discoveries and Inventions

Before proceeding to the main topic, let me touch upon the subject of liberating human nature. I would like you, who are studying the Truth, to know that the way your life unfolds and the way you change yourself by encountering the Truth depends on the day-to-day discoveries you make. Although it is easy to say that making discoveries is important, very few people actually remember this in their everyday lives. How to get closer to the core of the Truth and live more in tune with God's Will depends on your creative efforts and the new discoveries you make each day. This accumulation of discoveries is what ultimately adds depth to your soul. Life flows along quite monotonously for those who live each day without much thought, but for those who are actively accumulating discoveries every day, nothing else could be more exciting. If you have successfully discovered something new in the course of a day and take this as your personal challenge, you can say your day was worth living.

This is not something I am only asking of you; I myself make efforts every day to discover new things and invent new ways of doing things. For instance, this month (July

1988), I published five books, and people wondered how I managed to publish so many books in such a short period of time. The answer lies in my constant effort to find new ways of doing things. How did I manage to write five books in one month? Writing so many manuscripts by hand would be impossible. Some writers dictate their work, but this method would allow you to write perhaps one book a month at most. When I write a book, I first outline the chapters and sections and then speak based on the outline. So the transcript of my talk ends up being a complete manuscript of my book. Usually, the transcribed draft of a speech needs to be edited; the text needs to be proofread, split into paragraphs, or deleted. However, because my talks are based on a set outline, my books can be published at this speed. This process does not solely rely on spiritual guidance; it requires the effort and ingenuity of the person living in this world. You, too, can accomplish a great deal if you put in sufficient effort and find new ways of doing things.

Now, let me move on to the subject of this lecture, "the Principle of Salvation." As you launch a movement to save people, the challenge you will likely face is understanding that taking action under a slogan alone is not sufficient. The logic of business applies to the world of Truth, too. The world of business demands a constant increase in quality and quantity. A conflict exists between this demand and the ability of an individual to meet the demand. On the other hand, the idea of innovation has not been used to its full potential in religious circles or the world of Truth. So, in this sense, being creative and making new discoveries as you learn and convey the Truth to other people is essential. The outdated methods used by various other religious groups to convey the teachings lack creativity and may therefore be insufficient to launch a movement to truly save people. Doing "cookie-cutter" missionary work is not enough. Each person lives in a different environment, engages in different work, holds a different position, and has a different amount of time available. Under such circumstances, how can you convey the Truth?

If the Truth is indeed the Truth, it has the innate tendency to spread on its own. Then, how will you allow this impulse for propagation to manifest itself within your given situation? Although this is a very difficult challenge, you could discover hundreds of creative ways to convey the Truth to others if you put your mind to it. These ways may depend on your occupation, your gender, and the region in which you live, but each of you will have your own inventions and discoveries. If you work in a downtown office, for example, you could find fitting ways to study and spread the Truth within your business circles. If you are a homemaker, you can find your own ways to contribute to conveying the

Truth. As you can see in my books of spiritual messages, the power of women is considered a valuable force and has high expectations associated with it. One could say there are effective methods of conveying the Truth that is unique to women. If you live in the countryside, again, there must be a unique way to spread my teachings. Through constant efforts within the context of your unique occupation, position, and environment, you can certainly discover new and original ways to convey the Truth.

Then, how are these new methods devised? Where does this creativity express itself? I would like to look at this from two angles. First, creativity is necessary for establishing methods to control your own mind. In simple terms, the teaching of exploring the Right Mind ultimately means you will be blessed with a richer life once you are able to rule and control your own mind. Note that I am speaking in general about a variety of situations, so what I say may not always apply to your specific situation. Therefore, some level of creativity is required on an individual level to discover ways to use and apply these general teachings to solve your own specific problems. I published a book with answers to life's questions that I received from my readers; in it, you may find some problems similar to your own. But no two problems are exactly alike. It is an interesting challenge to find out how you can control your own mind using these materials as guides. Learning does not happen only during lectures and seminars. It also involves discovering ways to apply the teachings to your own problems. Only when you have tackled your own problems and overcome your own suffering or sense of unhappiness will you be convincing enough when you talk to others about what you have learned.

At this point, you will face the next challenge. Although you have succeeded in controlling your own mind and are filled with a sense of happiness, when you talk to others, you will find that their situations are quite different. So next comes the question of whether the lessons you have learned through your own experiences can be directly applied to others, which is another difficult challenge. This is where problems often occur for existing religious groups. People who belong to religions tend to think their experiences are the best and try to apply those experiences to others in the same way because they believe they have a cure-all. As a result, they fail or are disliked by others. This is a common pattern. Therefore, finding a way to overcome this hurdle is necessary. To this end, it is very important to first understand other people. You need to be able to see what the person is thinking about, his or her background and experiences, and what he or she wants.

Initially, your learning will be limited to the issues that apply to your situation. But once you get to the stage where you start applying the lessons from your life to the circumstances of others, you will begin to find creative ways to bring happiness not only into your own life but also into the lives of others. This will undoubtedly make other people happy, but you, yourself, will also experience even greater happiness. This is similar to how reading a novel allows you to gain experiences you have not actually experienced. Devising new ways to apply the Truth to someone who has experiences that are different from yours helps you gain lessons or nourishment for your own soul. So if you succeed in creatively guiding someone who is a completely different type of person than yourself, it would be the same as living two lives at once.

2

Live a Highly Efficient and Fulfilling Life

When we are born into this world, each of us chooses the most suitable environment for the development of our souls. Although your environment suits you the best, it may not provide you with every possible experience. Even if you were to frequently change jobs throughout your lifetime, you could only have at the most 20 or 30 different jobs. It is also not possible to be born as both man and woman. The same applies to other issues such as disease, poverty, and unemployment. One person cannot suffer from hundreds of different diseases within a single lifetime. Even when a person loses their job, because different types of businesses have different ways of working, the lessons they learn in each situation are different. When you look at life this way, you will notice that no matter how complicated an environment you chose to be born into, the number of lessons you can learn in a lifetime is limited. In general, people are reborn into this world approximately once every 300 years. Souls at higher spiritual levels such as bodhisattvas of the seventh dimension reincarnate once every 800–1,000 years. Souls at the tathagata level of the eighth dimension take between

1,000 and 2,000 years to be reborn. Being born into this world is a rare event. Therefore, whether you win in this life depends on how many lessons you learn and take back with you to the other world. Accordingly, you will quite naturally come to consider how to live a highly efficient and fulfilling life.

Rather than being satisfied with just solving your own life problems, if possible, why not try to solve the workbook of problems assigned to other people as well? Gain the strength to apply what you learn to solve a wide range of life's problems. Through this effort, you will be able to accumulate great wisdom, or *Prajna-Paramita*, as nourishment for your soul. Accordingly, it is necessary to be "selfish" in the truest sense. The selfishness I speak of here does not mean to assert yourself at the cost of others; it means to make the most of the several decades of life you are given and maximize what you gain. Being selfish in the truest sense is like harvesting as many crops as possible from a single acre of land. This does not go against God's Will by any means.

When applying the Truth to solve others' problems, you must think about how best to translate the Truth in a way others can understand and how best to offer words that revitalize others. This effort contains boundless potential and opens up a path to the infinite development of your soul. This is why there is no limit when studying the Truth. There may be a limit as long as you study the Truth only as knowledge, but once you reach the stage of applying this knowledge in life, all limits disappear. What you learn will transform and take an infinite number of forms.

This is the essence of the Laws. The Laws are not fixed; they are completely free, versatile, and ever-changing. Just as a stream of water flows into a great river, evaporates, forms clouds, and then falls as rain to form a stream once again, the Laws continue to change and take on many different forms as they nourish and enrich people's hearts and minds. This free and flexible nature of the Laws is known as the "egolessness of all phenomena" in Buddhism.

The Laws have no particular characteristic of their own. Although they may take a certain form at a particular time, in truth, they are always changing and warming people's hearts in many different ways.

3

Earth Is a Training Ground for Your Soul

To illustrate how the Laws assume different forms to guide people, I would like to take some examples from the lives of those who live on other planets. As Jesus, Moses, and other spirits mentioned in their spiritual messages conveyed in my books, we, who live on Earth, are not the only race; there are other beings in this great universe. Among them are beings who have a more advanced culture than ours as well as others who have a less developed culture. Various cultures suitable to each planet and the souls residing there are evolving.

In his spiritual message, Masaharu Taniguchi spoke about the wonders of time he learned in the Real World. His philosophy of "Eternal Now" has been developed further after his death. In it, he mentioned: "For those of us living on Earth, one year consists of 365 days, or the time it takes our planet to revolve around the Sun, and one day consists of 24 hours, or the time it takes Earth to rotate on its own axis. What would happen if we were to go to another planet?" Imagine a planet that completes a revolution around its sun in just 50 days. Assuming a year with 50 days and 4 seasons, each season would only last for about 10 days. Summer would last for about 10 days until autumn arrives, with just a couple of days between the two seasons. In no time, the leaves would fall, followed by snowfall. After another 10 days, spring would arrive. This would be a full year. If people lived in such a place, their lives would consist of very short cycles; they would be living an extremely fast-paced life.

What types of souls would live on such a planet? Even on our planet, there are two different types of people—those who work at a hectic pace and those who live in a leisurely way. Some people are extremely busy working and accomplishing a great deal, thereby accumulating a wide variety of experiences in a single lifetime. When these souls have very little left to learn here, they will most likely reincarnate on a planet where time passes in extremely short cycles. On Earth, they might be able to work five or ten times as fast as others, but when they go to a planet where a year is only 50 days, they will appear to be very slow. Their rhythm of life and pace of work will seem like a video in slow motion. Others on that planet will work much more quickly and think much faster than them. To keep up with the people on that planet, the newcomers from Earth will have to make a great deal of effort, thus moving to the next stage of their spiritual development.

The opposite type of people on Earth, who appreciate the philosophy of leisure of Lao-tzu and Chuang-tzu, are the ones who may come to our lectures on Sundays but otherwise stay at home and spend their time meditating. Such people may think they lead the most leisurely life possible. But what if they go to a planet where a year consists of a thousand days? On some planets, "sloth-like people" have an even slower pace of life. Here, even the act of having a meal is very slow. When you sit down at the table, for example, you might stare at the cutlery for 5 or 10 minutes and consider how it should be used before taking the first morsel. When certain people are reincarnated on such a planet, they may realize how hectic their seemingly leisurely lives on Earth had actually been. They may discover that even when meditating, they had been bound by the idea of meditation and that they cannot complete their spiritual development unless they can live in a more relaxed way, free from all thought. They may think they still have a long way to go before they achieve a state of oneness with nature. Thus, many planets in this universe have a different pace of life, and they all have their own type of spiritual discipline suitable for the souls living there.

Some planets also have a heavily one-sided ratio of male to female inhabitants. I have a lot of information regarding this and would like to speak about it as part of my teachings on the universe someday. For example, on a planet with only 10 percent female population, women are extremely fertile and can give birth to five or six children at a time. Like queen bees, they can bear dozens of children in a lifetime, and they possess great authority and reign over others as if they were sun goddesses. When these women become too accustomed to wielding power and grow arrogant, they are sent to another planet like Earth, where women are considered to be created from Adam's rib. There, they must take on further spiritual training.

Although initially you choose an environment that is appropriate for your spiritual growth, through the many cycles of reincarnation in the same environment, your soul develops particular traits or tendencies. Eventually, you reach a point where you can no longer develop within that environment. Of course, you may be able to grow a little when times change, but in economic terms, "the marginal utility" of the lessons your soul can learn is considerably diminished. The amount of nourishment a soul can acquire in a single lifetime becomes very limited. When this happens, the human soul chooses to be born in an environment that is either completely different or is far more extreme so that their tendencies can be developed further.

As you may have learned from my other books, Earth was formed about 4.6 billion years ago when a part of the Sun split off from its main body. This part orbited the Sun until it gradually cooled down and became habitable for living creatures. The creation of the Sun and Earth was part of

God's plan to create a living environment that was different from the other planets.

Then, roughly 365 million years ago, beings similar to humans were invited to live on Earth from Planet Zeta in the Magellanic Clouds. You may recall that in one of my books, a spirit said that Zeta and Earth have different ratios of land and sea and that the two have slightly different environments. The soul tendency of the people from Zeta was that they were quite advanced in the scientific sense.

Right now, we must go through the hassle of preparing for an event; I, too, must travel to get to the venue. But with further scientific advancements, I could give a lecture to everyone across the country while I lie down at home. If our technology evolves even further, perhaps I could wear a device on my head that will allow me to send my ideas to all of you as soon as I think of them. This could be possible. At this stage, you will be able to harvest fewer experiences for your soul. Human souls strive to grow infinitely, but at some point, they will no longer be able to learn as much as they used to. So some souls from Zeta who wished to start over in a new environment decided to leave their planet of advanced science. This is how they began their life on Earth, a planet without many scientific advancements at the time of their immigration.

Many different beings from other planets have immigrated to Earth after intervals of a few hundred million years. Many souls have come here from other planets to become earthlings, and Earth has been serving as a new training ground for them.

4

The Splitting of Souls and God's Will

This is not to say that all human souls have migrated from other planets; some souls have originated on Earth. You may have already learned about the theory of the core spirit and branch spirits. According to this theory, about 70–80 percent of the people living now have souls that were created on Earth. Let me explain how these souls are created. First, a model core spirit is chosen; then, the spiritual energy from the tenth dimensional divine spirit that governs the development on Earth, also called the Grand Sun Consciousness, is applied to the core spirit to significantly increase its energy level. For example, when I was reviewing the video of my first lecture, "The Principle of Happiness" in 1987, I noticed I was skinny and my face looked pointy. Now, a year later, I must be feeling more comfortable given how my face has gotten rounder. If I gain more weight, I might feel like I could split myself into two people. I could continue to become as big as a sumo wrestler and then I might feel like splitting myself into four people. Similarly, in the world of souls, when the energy level of a soul significantly increases, remaining as a single entity is difficult, and the soul becomes capable of splitting itself.

One of the basic patterns of soul splitting is the model used in the sixth dimension, where five branch spirits are produced by copying one sixth dimensional high spirit as the core spirit. This will result in six times as many spirits, and this is the basic pattern. The souls at higher spiritual levels can split themselves more freely. According to the spirit of Immanuel Kant, "one is many and many are one." Confucius, in his spiritual message, said he is capable of splitting into 10,000 or even 100 million entities. In terms of energy, because the amount of energy that can be contained within one physical body is limited, spirits that embody vast amounts of energy can split themselves into many individual souls.

The Japanese books of history, *Kojiki* and *Nihon-Shoki*, recount many mythological tales of how different gods were born. For example, when a god was washing his ears in a river, another god was born from those ears; the same thing happened when he washed his eyes and mouth. According to these tales, both males and females are capable of giving birth. Although it sounds very mystical, this story symbolically illustrates how energy can be split to create more souls. In this way, many different types of soul groups are among us and train on Earth. Many of the angels who created the history of humankind belonged to the main soul group created by El Cantare. Therefore, there are the mainstream souls and the ones who later immigrated to Earth. A group of souls was also created on Earth to increase the number of spirits.

Why is it necessary for one spirit to split into many, like a core spirit and the five or six branch spirits? This is actually the expression of supreme happiness. The fact that one person can achieve happiness is a wonderful thing. It is also wonderful for that one person to develop greatness of character by attaining enlightenment. But imagine the joy of 5, 10, 100, 1,000, or even 10,000 people sharing that same experience. The joy would surely be extraordinary. Happiness is felt more powerfully when shared by many rather than when savored alone. This is God's intention.

In my book of spiritual messages from Masaharu Taniguchi, he says, "When you think of God, you have to interpret the two conflicting ideas of 'completion' and 'progress' as one. Otherwise, if you consider God to be absolutely perfect and complete, then there would be only stagnation in the world God created." It would be like a painting on a canvas that is perfect; there would be no need to add any finishing touches. If there is any room for alteration, you would not call it a completed work of art. However, the world God created is a world of energy. It is a world where this energy transforms in various ways and creates various phenomena. When we think of this world as a world of energy, one question arises: What is the state of perfection? Imagine a dam. If this dam can generate sufficient energy for the population of a particular region, should it be considered perfect? It may be perfect as a dam, but from the perspective of the energy it contains or the transformation and development of that energy, we cannot say the dam is perfect when it can only generate sufficient power for its immediate surroundings. Only when the dam is capable of supplying unlimited energy can it be considered close to the state of perfection.

Similarly, if God is considered perfect and complete in the world of souls or spiritual energy, God must be a supplier of infinite energy. This energy gushing forth must flow into many tributaries, each of which must become as vast as the main river. These newly created main streams must branch into tributaries again and create yet more main streams. Unless this happens, God cannot be considered perfect from the artistic perspective of energy. If God is satisfied with a single stream of energy, then one could say He is far from being complete.

From this we can infer the existence of God and His Will. God aims to achieve boundless harmony and limitless progress within infinite diversity and infinite individuality. Creating a society that only comprises a handful of people in harmony and making progress is not enough for Him. Quantitative limits do not exist in God's mind. He wishes for an infinite increase in beings, progress, and harmony and will not be satisfied until it is achieved. As the means to this end, God created "time."

5

God's Three Great Inventions

Creation of the world through will

My book *Starting from the Ordinary* (reprinted as *Twiceborn*) has a chapter titled "Existence and Time" that is unique and stands out from the rest of the book. You can read it as a standalone chapter and consider it as one philosophy. I believe the content of this chapter has surpassed that of *Being and Time* by Martin Heidegger. In my book, you can find this content written in simple language. The most important and magnificent of God's inventions is the creation of the world through will. Different things can be created using will. For example, human spirits, earth, stars, rivers, and oceans— these were all created by God's Will. In the spirit world, too, different kinds of buildings and beautiful landscapes were created using the power of will. This is God's first invention. The great wisdom of the universe made it possible to create the world and all the objects and phenomena in it through will. In the beginning, God had such an intention to create the world.

Creation of time

God's second intention was to place the things He created through will in a flow of time. This gave rise to "beings." For "beings" to evolve, the invention of "time" was essential. Although you may not have thought about it, "time" as we know it was also an invention. Imagine you were a being in a photograph that had been pasted onto a flat surface. Would you be satisfied with this kind of two-dimensional existence? If you were photographed, your image would appear in the photo and you would certainly exist in a two-dimensional plane. But no matter how long anyone stared at the picture, it would not change. What would it be like to just look at and appreciate the static image? Let's say I were the Creator and thought of creating a thousand human beings. Using the power of my own will, I created men and women wearing a variety of clothing. At first, I may feel delighted about successfully creating a variety of individuals. However, these beings without movement would be like pictures on a wall. Seeing them day after day, I would gradually become dissatisfied and grow bored because although these beings "exist," they do not move, develop, or change. Accordingly, this condition creates boredom and the desire to seek more ways for further development. As His first invention, God created the world and all the beings in it using His Will, but He was not satisfied; so next He created time.

Time is a framework that sets beings in motion. After His first invention—the rule of "creation through will"—God came up with the idea of allowing the world to unfold on its own and letting all beings develop by themselves. The time lag between the first invention and this second invention was just a moment in earthly time. But within that moment, time was invented, owing to which, beings were allowed to change their form. Without this invention, the universe would have remained completely stationary and all of us would have been static, so time was a truly great invention.

First, beings could be created using will. Then, those existences could enter a framework for development through the invention of time. In the flow of time, beings could continue to exist while they change themselves. This is how the two-step framework was created.

Creation of "the direction of happiness or progress"

Thus, God created beings and their framework for motion. What did He think of next? A direction. On seeing the beings changing themselves at will, God felt something was missing in the fulfillment of His original intention. For example, if

God created a thousand humans and set the framework for motion, the humans could now cough, open a book, fix a tie, or do whatever they wished to do. But all these random actions alone were not satisfactory for their development. Therefore, God thought of giving them a direction for their framework for motion. This led Him to His third invention: the concept of happiness or progress. Progress and happiness are like two sides of the same coin; the concepts of happiness and progress, which we can also call prosperity, are very similar to each other. Then, God gave the beings that had been endowed with motion a direction—to make progress with the goal of achieving happiness.

In fact, this great universe consists of these three inventions. Our existence and our life lie within the flow of these inventions. We can view ourselves from this perspective.

6

Gratitude for God's Inventions

In my book *Kofuku Meiso Ho* (literally, "The Methods of Meditation for Happiness"), I teach a meditation method for people to be content or to develop the "it's enough mind." I talk about how wonderful and pleasant it is to be a human being. For instance, would you be happy as a dog, a cat, a plant, or a pebble? If you imagine yourself in a non-human form and view your current self from that perspective, you will understand how extremely fortunate you are. If you were a flower such as a Saintpaulia, an African violet, you would not be able to speak. If you were a dog, your happiness would be limited to going for a walk. If you were a cat, climbing a tree might have given you happiness. These beings may have other forms of happiness, but their happiness is limited. So you must realize how lucky you are to be a human and learn to be content. This is a very important concept, and I want to delve deeper into it.

Gratitude for the "creation of the world through will"

I want you to think about yourself in light of God's three great inventions. First, think about what a great blessing it is to come into being in this universe. Our existence here and now indicates that there is a will allowing us to exist. We exist as a result of a will that says, "Be this way." The Creator of the universe has enough power to make all human beings disappear in an instant if He wished to. Not only that, it might be easy for Him to make the entire earth disappear. God can easily create or destroy. We are beings that can easily appear or disappear according to His Will. Nevertheless, we are allowed to live each day, so we must be grateful for God's first rule, His first invention. It is a surprise and a delight to realize we are allowed to exist because of God's Will.

You may think animals are the only non-humans with souls, but from a spiritual perspective, plants also have souls. Each flower has its own unique colors and patterns, which are the expression of the lovely soul residing within.

You may think it ends with animals and plants, but minerals also have souls. The souls of minerals progress slowly; one year for a human being may correspond to a million or even a hundred million years for minerals. Take, for example, a diamond. Coal turns into a diamond when tremendous pressure is applied to it. Diamonds are formed deep underground where such pressure exists. They emerge to the surface with the movement of Earth's crust or through volcanic eruptions and are used to make jewelry. I do not know the length of this entire process, but the diamonds are living their own life. Minerals live for extremely long periods of time that are beyond our imagination.

In fact, the transformation of carbon into diamond is a new birth. The crystallization of a diamond is the equivalent of the birth of a human being. This period of transformation is very long compared with the human pregnancy period; nevertheless, crystallization is similar to birth for them. A diamond has a life of its own and follows a certain process until it is born, just like a human baby. A newly formed diamond crystal gradually increases in size; this is the equivalent of human growth. It then emerges to the surface of Earth to be used in various ways, similar to how young people enter the working world. Thus, minerals too have their own life history and soul, which is different from ours but enables them to form mineral crystals. These souls are very static, but they have the power to create crystals; diamonds form diamond crystals, rubies form ruby crystals, sapphires form sapphire crystals, and quartz form quartz crystals. This can never happen by accident. A particular type of power that attracts specific atoms and molecules to form crystals exists. These life forms, which are more primitive than animals and plants, were also created.

Thus, understanding the significance of the fact that all beings are created by God's Will is important. Moreover, we must know that nothing was created by accident; every being or object exists only because there is a will that says "Be this way," allowing it to exist.

Gratitude for the "creation of time"

Next, we need to be grateful for God's second invention, time. Thanks to the creation of time, we are able to live; without time, we would be completely motionless, like mannequins. There would be no happiness under such conditions, so we must appreciate the existence of time and savor the happiness.

It is unclear why human beings have a life span of several decades to a hundred years. But this is probably the optimum length of time for our souls to develop. Why does a dog only live for 10 or 15 years? Some dogs and cats only live for two or three years. A cicada lives underground for several years and has a week to live above ground. Each creature is given its appropriate life span; there is a being who decided that each creature would have a certain life span for its spiritual development. We need to think about the significance of this.

I once read a story in a book of fairy tales about a man who attained immortality through magic or some potion and was fairly happy until he was about a hundred years old. However, he experienced the deaths of his friends and family one after another while he remained young for another 500 years, then 1,000 years. Ironically, this story shows the pain and unhappiness that we would experience if we were unable to die. As humans, we long for eternal life; at the same time, as part of our nature, we dislike stagnation. We die with age. Many people are probably afraid of dying. However, to be able to die after having lived out the span of one's life is quite fortunate. Just as a cicada sheds its shell to be born anew, through death, our souls are given another opportunity to continue developing. The fact that we are given the opportunity to take another step forward is, in itself, an expression of mercy. Please think about the greatness of this mercy, the greatness of this love that allows us to be reborn again and again and to experience different lives. In this way, I would like you to cherish the happiness that the creation of time brings in regard to our life span; we can live because time allows our planet Earth to rotate on its own axis in 24 hours and revolve around the Sun in 365 days.

Gratitude for the "creation of the direction of happiness or progress"

The third invention leads us to learn the "it's enough mind." I would like you to think about how blessed we are that God gave us the direction of pursuing greater happiness within the framework of developing in the universe. What if the goal of motion had been destruction, extinction, death, or depletion? What would happen to this world? It would be a very dark place. Earlier, I talked about selfishness. Selfishness can become evil in relationships with others, but the fact that every human being, animal, and plant innately want to live a richer life is an expression of great mercy and something for us to be thankful for. If every life form had only self-destructive urges, this world would be a terrible place to live. The stress of civilization tends to drive humans to wage wars, but if human souls were created with an innate desire to kill when they come of age, what would this world be like? For example, imagine a rule mandating young people to kill their parents who had brought them up upon reaching the age of 20. Our world could have been like this, but thanks to God, it was not created in such a way. This is something for us to be very happy about. If we had been created with an innate tendency to kill everyone we meet, what a terrible world we would live in. Fortunately, however, we have the desire to develop and become happy. It goes without saying that this desire is common in a world beyond language—that is, in the deepest part of our minds. We need to be aware of how blessed we are to have been created in this way.

7

The Reincarnation of Stars and Planets

So far, I have discussed time. Next, I would like to talk about space. Space is also a great blessing. Thanks to the current size of Earth and its gravitational field, we are able to live in our present physical bodies. If Earth was compressed under enormous pressure and turned into a ball that was less than 1.77 cm (0.7 in) in diameter, what would happen? It would become a black hole. If the size of Earth was slightly larger than that of a button, all the heat and light that radiate from it would be sucked inward, and the space around it would be distorted.

Just as human beings repeatedly reincarnate, stars and planets also go through reincarnation. We are now living in the third dimensional world, and the human spirits inhabit the fourth, fifth, sixth, seventh, eighth, and ninth dimensional worlds. I have mentioned that the ninth dimension is the highest level a human spirit can attain; this dimension currently has 10 spirits, each with different characteristics. Beyond this is the tenth dimension, where planetary consciousnesses exist, namely the Grand Sun Consciousness, the Moon Consciousness, and the Earth Consciousness. As a planetary consciousness, each planet, be it Earth, the Moon, Jupiter, or Venus, has its own soul and cycle of reincarnation; viewed from a broader perspective, these souls also reincarnate. The time it takes for a planetary consciousness to reincarnate is not constant. Taking the example of the planetary systems of the Milky Way, the average cycle of reincarnation for a planet is approximately 15 billion years. Within this cycle, a planetary consciousness reincarnates, so the planet experiences physical death at some point.

The death of a planet is when it becomes a black hole. In the course of a planet's lifespan, it can split into pieces and die as the result of an accident, like a collision or explosion, but it can also die a natural death at the end of its lifespan. When planets die naturally, they turn into black holes; this is a telltale sign of a dying planet. This generally happens about 15 billion years after a planet's birth. Take Earth, for example. Fifteen billion years after its creation, it will begin to decay as a living entity. To the Earth Consciousness, the massive sphere called Earth is its physical body or one massive cell. Just as a human spirit resides in a physical body, which ages and dies after 80 years or so, the Earth Consciousness resides in a physical planet that will also eventually die. For a planet, the most common form of death is turning into a black hole; in other words, the volume of the planet becomes extremely small—a planet with a circumference of tens of thousands of kilometers (tens of thousands of miles) contracts until its circumference is about a couple of centimeters (less than an inch). This is the stage of death for a planet. At this stage, its soul or planetary consciousness is contracting to one point and finishing its mission. After the planet contracts to one point, it disintegrates and disappears.

Then, what happens to its soul? The huge planetary consciousness becomes very small—it becomes as small as a human soul entering a mother's womb. It then enters the next phase. The soul, which has become as small as a human embryo, enters the basis for the new planet-to-be. Planets are born in many ways; some are born after splitting away from a star, whereas others are born as a natural phenomenon. In the latter case, the process of gases and cosmic dust gathering, condensing, and repeatedly exploding creates a new planet. A soul that has gone through the black hole stage becomes the core of this phenomenon. Once a soul reaches this stage, it enters a state of sleep and loses consciousness, exactly like a human soul entering the embryo stage. With this soul as the core, many different natural phenomena start to occur around it; a vortex of gases begins to form, and a centripetal force gradually develops and begins to attract various elements. Then, a new planet is born.

As I mentioned earlier, the average cycle of reincarnation for a planet is about 15 billion years. Accordingly, Earth will continue to exist for quite a while. However, this is only if it undergoes a natural death. Earth can also possibly experience some peculiar circumstances in which it internally splits or collides with another celestial body and breaks into pieces. The tenth dimensional consciousnesses determine these cycles and make the necessary adjustments.

8

The Words for Saving

Today, I discussed from different perspectives the changes humans and souls go through in this great universe. When returning to our starting point and thinking about the principle of salvation, the most important point is to understand the universe and human existence. Without an understanding of these fundamental topics, spreading the Truth will be pointless. Why are we spreading the Truth? Is it merely to advertise our group, Happy Science? Will gaining more members satisfy us? Is this what our activities are all about? We must not misunderstand the starting point of our activities. We must first fully understand our main purpose; only then can we proceed with our specific and concrete activities.

Human beings were created by God

Then, what do we have to convey to others, including people in other religious groups and those who have no wish to know about the soul or God? First, we must tell them about God's first invention: the creation of the universe, human beings, and all life through the Will of God. We need to put this first Truth into our own words and convey it to others. Some people believe they are living in this world by chance. They think they were randomly thrown into this world and were born by chance into an unfamiliar environment. They believe everything will be over when they die. However, this materialistic view of life clearly goes against God's first invention. It is a view held by the people who do not know how this world was really created. We need to tell these people the true view of life by putting it into our own words.

By learning that we are creations of God, we can nurture each other and awaken to true gratitude for the first time. As long as people view life as the by-product of an accident, they cannot appreciate the happiness or gratitude that arises when cooperating with others. For this reason, explaining God's first invention to these people in your own words is important. The existence of the spirit and the body is attributable to this first invention. In fact, the world of matter was created through the process of transforming spiritual energy into matter. You may have already read this in *Spiritual Messages from Edison*. It is necessary to explain God's first invention and the phenomena caused by it to others.

The meaning of time

Next is God's second invention—time. We must teach others about the meaning of time. Time has two meanings. The first has to do with our individual lives. We need to inform people how best to use the time we are given in this life and how to create time that contains the value of Truth.

My book *Starting from the Ordinary* has a chapter titled "Existence and Time" that presents the two different types of time that we live in: relative time and absolute time. "Relative" time is the time that can be measured objectively with a clock. If I give a public lecture for 75 minutes, for example, those 75 minutes will be the same for every listener. However, depending on how much Truth a person assimilates in those 75 minutes, this span of time can expand infinitely. For some people, this experience is equivalent to living an infinite time. I call this kind of time that contains the value of Truth "absolute" time. We live in these two types of time—absolute time and relative time. This is a development of Einstein's theory of relativity in relation to the Truth. Relative time and absolute time exist in the space of Truth. This is the law of physics applied to the realm of Truth.

The second meaning of time has to do with the significance of the times humans are living in now. We must think about this. By understanding the significance of our age—the end of the 20th century—and what it signifies in the context of the long history of humankind, we will come to realize the need to change the way we live. This is not a time when we can be satisfied just to lead mediocre lives. Nostradamus' prophecies describe the tragic events in our future, but neither am I sure of when exactly and how these events will unfold nor do I wish to find out. I just know for a fact that a time of misfortune, tragedy, and destruction is drawing near. The high spirits in heaven are in a hurry to have their teachings published. Why? Please understand that there is a reason for this. If you do not, it means you have not seen or sensed anything. We are publishing many books of Truth as quickly as possible because we are in a rush. The time is coming. But before it does, we want to light up the torch of Truth. We want to establish the basics of the Truth, lay its foundations, and spread it. Please sense the meaning behind the urgency of our activities. We are living at the turning point of humanity; this perspective is another criterion for using your time.

Happiness as our goal

Finally, we must faithfully follow God's third invention: the goal called happiness. The goal of humanity is certainly not the survival of just one person or that of just one nation or society. The goal is to realize infinite harmony and infinite progress. From the very beginning, God has told us to pursue infinite happiness while embracing all kinds of individuality and diversity. Without this purpose of happiness, there can be no movement for salvation.

To sum up, the movement for salvation must include three aspects: God's Will that allows all beings to exist, the creation of time, and the goal of happiness. I, myself, also hope to move forward based on this idea.

CHAPTER FOUR

The Principle of
Self-Reflection

The Fourth Public Lecture of 1988

Originally recorded in Japanese on October 2, 1988
at Tokyo Metropolitan Hibiya Public Hall in Tokyo, Japan
and later translated into English.

1

The Meaning of Self-Reflection

In our movement of spreading the Truth, which began with the publication of a series of spiritual messages, we have now sold over one million copies (at the time of this lecture). This number will soon grow to two, five, and ten million copies and create a surge that I believe will reach all over Japan. Now, where do you think you are currently swimming in the flow of the growing number of books and the diverse Laws? Are you just drifting? Have you managed to successfully swim through it? I suspect many of you have not been able to evaluate your situation. However, I want to emphasize that most importantly, you have to establish yourself. Now that we have started seeing potential growth, we need to pull ourselves together again, reflect deeply on ourselves, and establish ourselves to grow and progress further.

In my book *The Essence of Buddha*, I have revealed exactly what the thoughts of Shakyamuni Buddha, who lived in India about 2,600 years ago, were in a way that is easy to understand. I condensed his thoughts into a framework that forms the very essence of Buddhism. No matter how many Buddhist scriptures you read—tens of thousands or more—if you cannot understand the thoughts described in

The Essence of Buddha, you have not truly grasped Buddhism. In other words, all of Shakyamuni Buddha's teachings during his 81 years of life are condensed into the framework of his thoughts. I do plan to write a book on his life in detail at some point, but I decided to first clarify the essence or the framework of his thoughts in *The Essence of Buddha*. So, what did Buddha want to teach? The content of the book can be expressed in a single statement: "Understand the meaning of self-reflection."

You may wonder "why?" What is self-reflection for? Do we practice it just because that is the right thing to do? Or does the act of self-reflection itself have some significant meaning? Is there a more profound significance that we are not yet aware of? You may ask yourself these questions. Because I have been born with the destiny to see what people cannot see, hear what people cannot hear, and know things people usually do not know, I must teach you a very important fact. Although you may think you are in control of your life and in charge of more than 99 percent of your thoughts and actions, this is not necessarily the case. In the world that is invisible to your eyes, various phenomena occur. Moreover, people's happiness or unhappiness is generally determined by the influence of spiritual beings. The majority of today's global population—about five billion (at the time of this lecture)—is unaware that they are under the influence of spiritual beings. This is a very difficult fact for me to accept. You must awaken; you must understand that even if you think you are in control of your own life, you may actually be living like a puppet.

Let me explain in detail. Most people I have met are to some extent under some kind of spiritual influence. Very few seem to be under the good influence or under the influence of their guardian and guiding spirits. The majority is exposed to negative spiritual vibrations at certain times of the day, although the duration and extent of this exposure differ from person to person. This phenomenon is common for all people. As children of God, indeed, this is a disgraceful sight for us. Human beings, who are considered the lords of creation, are often influenced by animal spirits or lost spirits in various ways. When I see humans allowing their lives to be manipulated by the ill will of these spirits and falling into an abyss, I am all the more determined to eliminate these negative influences. I want each person to live every day thinking, "I have lived today with my true self."

Many of you are living lives you can hardly call your own. You are just accepting the results of that life and bearing its responsibilities. You are drifting in this destiny. But as children of God, children of Buddha, you need to awaken. How much longer are you going to let yourself be misled by these negative influences? Wake up immediately to the awareness of being a child of God; shine your noble, divine nature. The time has come. The way to do this is very simple: self-reflection—a method that has repeatedly been taught to people since 2,000 years ago, 3,000 years ago, or even longer ago.

2

Ra Mu's Threefold Path

More than 16,000 years ago, on an ancient continent called Mu, which has since disappeared without a trace, was a person named Ra Mu. He taught people about self-reflection. He repeatedly said, "Get back your true self. To do so, break free from negative materialistic vibrations and calm your disturbed state of mind." I can see such visions of him in various forms with my mind's eye. Many high spirits have frequently come down to this world to teach and guide people in various ways. However, throughout all of it, one teaching has always remained the same, unchanged, and undistorted: "You must correct the mistakes in your mind with your own will. That is when the great river of destiny will flow in the direction you are heading." As one of the methods to do so, Shakyamuni Buddha taught the Eightfold Path. But Ra Mu's teachings were different. If compared to the Eightfold Path, his teaching could be called the Threefold Path.

The first step in Ra Mu's Threefold Path was self-reflection on love. Ra Mu taught that you must live with love for others and reflect every day on whether you gave love to others.

The second step was whether you can attune your mind to God or the guardian and guiding spirits who are close to God today. Ra Mu taught that if you are unable to hear the voice of your guardian and guiding spirits, either directly or indirectly, this means your mind is clouded and the clouds are obstructing you from hearing them. If you cannot turn your mind to the heavenly world, the cause lies in your thoughts and actions during the day. Therefore, you need to reflect on them.

Ra Mu's third teaching was about reflecting on what you learned today. Evaluate whether you have not wasted your day. Life is only a matter of decades. But to be born in this world and into the environment and circumstances you are in now is not easy. Unless you have extremely good luck, you cannot be born at this age. So do not waste your life away. Do not waste this year. Do not waste this day. Ra Mu strongly emphasized this point. Learn from every experience. Do not go a day without learning, not even an hour, a minute, or a second.

You may think of the Eightfold Path as a definitive method of self-reflection. But self-reflection actually is the attitude of not wasting the time we have been given in our lives. As long as this understanding is at the basis of self-reflection, it can be practiced in infinite ways.

I am now teaching the True Eightfold Path. I have reframed Shakyamuni Buddha's teachings in a modern context using simple language so that each one of you knows his teachings. However, there are infinite methods to self-reflect, and I am yet to teach many other methods. These methods depend on whether you have awakened to your spirituality and to what degree.

As a starting point, I would like to recommend Ra Mu's Threefold Path, which is much easier to practice than the Eightfold Path. The three criteria are relatively easy to practice. The first criterion is to see if you have given love to others today. Human beings are natural givers of love. Therefore, if you do not give love, you will be going against your true nature. You must first reflect on this. The second criterion, in short, is to reflect on whether you had a peaceful mind. If you are unable to communicate with your guardian and guiding spirits, this means the vibrations of your mind are disturbed. So calm the vibrations of your mind and make daily efforts to be peaceful. The third criterion is to reflect on what you have learned. This self-reflection is for you to build a more positive self.

Many people mistakenly think that self-reflection is simply the process of looking back to the past, but the true purpose of self-reflection is to correct your thoughts and actions and therefore create a more constructive life. You must not think of self-reflection simply as a passive practice. You must not think that its purpose is only to cancel out the negatives in your life. The true purpose of self-reflection is to develop a more positive self and realize God's Will in the name of building utopia in this world. Under this purpose, the difference between self-reflection and prayer can be disregarded. We should not concentrate solely on the method and lose sight of the essence. We must wish to change our current selves for the better and take actions that produce more wonderful outcomes. The essence of self-reflection and prayer can be summarized into this single purpose.

The three self-reflection methods I just talked about are very easy to practice, and I believe you can immediately start practicing them. However, some complicated elements are involved in self-reflection. For example, you may have unfortunately been unable to experience the effects of self-reflection. Very few people probably understand the power of self-reflection. Its power is remarkable; with my spiritual sight, I can see evil spirits or a cluster of thoughts possessing a person falling off as soon as he or she starts self-reflecting as if the ropes that were attached to them have been cut off. I would like you to understand the amount of power that exists in the act of self-reflection.

3

Manifest Your Divine Nature Within

Now, I must tell you a fact about divine light. You may think light is something we receive from the outside or is given to us by other-power. You may tend to think that the high spiritual beings bestow light and that you receive salvation through this light. This idea certainly contains some truth. In my book *Ai kara Inori e* (literally, "From Love to Prayers"), I have taught the different ways to pray and introduced many prayers. When you verbally recite the prayers, you become a spiritual source emitting spiritual energy or vibrations and create a golden bridge to the higher spiritual world. In some cases, various guiding spirits give you power; you may certainly experience this.

However, I am giving the lecture on "The Principle of Self-Reflection" before "The Principle of Prayer" because I want to tell you that light does not always come from the outside. The essence of self-reflection that Shakyamuni Buddha taught is that "light shines from within."

People who have practiced meditation in Happy Science seminars have probably experienced full moon meditation—a practice in which you visualize a full moon. Full moon meditation is not merely a meditation practice;

it shows you the state that you can ultimately achieve when you thoroughly pursue self-reflection. I, myself, also practice self-reflection. When I look within myself and sink deep into my mind, I can see an image of myself. This image is not of my physical body. I see myself as a golden statue of Buddha. From within the lower abdomen of this golden statue, I can clearly see light being emitted. Full moon meditation actually shows you the completed form of self-reflection.

When you practice self-reflection, you probably examine the thoughts that cross your mind one by one. Unless you see this shining self-image as you enter a state of deep meditation, your self-reflection is not complete. When your self-reflection is complete, your whole body will emit light, called an aura or a halo. However, this light does not just shine on the outside; with spiritual sight, your whole body should look like a golden statue. Moreover, it should disperse intense light in all directions from the inside. This is when I sense the existence of light different from the one we experience during prayer. The light during prayer comes down from high above, whereas the light from self-reflection shines from within.

Only when you see and know this will you truly be able to understand the structure of the mind, which I have taught in the book *Shin Kokoro no Tankyu* (literally, "The Exploration of the Mind: New Version") and other books. In these books,

I have explained that the structure of our mind is layered like an onion. In every human mind, the fourth, fifth, sixth, seventh, eighth, ninth, and tenth dimensions exist in layers like an onion. You will ultimately come to know this truth through self-reflection.

At the center of the human mind is the core that connects to the Real World and even to the world beyond where human souls live. The eighth or ninth dimension is said to be the highest dimension that human souls can reach, but a part within us receives light from the tenth dimension, the eleventh dimension, and even beyond. A point at the deepest, most profound part of our mind is ultimately connected to God, who exists in the deepest part of the great universe. When you become aware of this, it is important to know that there are ways to seek that light within.

After all, this is what Shakyamuni Buddha mainly tried to teach. When comparing the teachings of two great spiritual leaders, Jesus Christ and Shakyamuni Buddha, this point is exactly where a clear difference lies. Jesus Christ was aware that an absolute being who transcended him exists far beyond. He sometimes referred to this Being as "Father" and at other times as "God." He was aware that this transcendental existence is far greater than his soul dwelling in a physical body, and this was what he taught. This is the starting point of faith in other-power.

In contrast, Shakyamuni Buddha did not teach about other-power because he did not consider human beings or the souls that dwell in physical bodies as weak beings. In Jesus' teachings, human beings appear weak and fragile. Because people were sometimes treated as sinners, imagining them as weak individuals is easy. But in the eyes of Shakyamuni Buddha, human beings were truly strong. He saw strength at their very core. Of course, he had seen many people being washed away by the rough currents of destiny and being caught up in the vortex of karma. In this sense, Shakyamuni Buddha saw just as many fragile people as Jesus did. However, he had discovered God's Light at the core of every human being. This is why he did not intentionally teach faith. He did not consider faith as the act of revering something far away but taught people to awaken to the light or the core within themselves; he taught that everything would be there and that they would see everything and be given all the power. He held a worldview wherein the inner universe encompasses the outer universe. Only with such a perspective can faith gain more power and transform itself into even greater energy.

The inner self and the transcendental consciousness are not separate entities but are spiritual energy passing through the same point and sharing the same source. People who have fully grasped this fact can live life with much power, strength, and courage. In other words, instead of seeking help to escape from being weak, you need to realize you are not weak. God or Buddha is within you and you must discover that. You must awaken to God or Buddha and manifest the Buddha-nature that is within you. The teachings of Buddhism can be summarized as this single point. If you cannot understand or acknowledge this single truth, you have not learned or understood Buddhism yet. To what extent can you discover this fire, this flame, this light? This is your challenge.

4

The True Eightfold Path

1) Right View

When you look back and reflect upon your day, many thoughts may come to mind. Regarding the Eightfold Path, Right View comes first. Right View involves checking if you see things rightly or in the right manner. You may think this is a matter of course, but how many people actually check to see whether they are viewing things rightly? Right View has three checkpoints.

The first is how you view the people around you. People's suffering often comes from interpersonal problems, so checking whether you were able to view others and their ways in the right manner is important. Did you see others in the same way God sees them?

The second checkpoint is to assess how you see yourself. Were you easy on yourself today? Did you have a biased view of yourself? Were you overly lenient with yourself? Did you evaluate yourself rightly? Did you evaluate yourself in the same way God would have evaluated you? Or did you justify yourself based only on your own criteria? You must ask yourself these questions.

The last checkpoint is to assess the troubles you have with others. Incidents and conflicts occur when people interact with each other. Therefore, you have to evaluate whether you observed the incidents or conflicts that involved you rightly.

Right View includes these three perspectives. Only by reflecting on these checkpoints will the Buddha-nature that had been dormant within you gradually awaken. As you deepen your practice of Right View, the image or idea that you had of others will gradually change, and you will begin to think differently. You will be able to see both "the phenomenal self (which only temporarily appears)" and "the Buddha-nature-manifested self" and tell them apart.

How I see people and how you see them is clearly different. Can you point out this difference? Do you know how I view each and every one of you? What I see is the Light of God that lies within each of you. Your physical appearance—your skin, clothes, hair—is not what I see. I see how much of your true nature as the child of God you are manifesting; I see the state of this light within you. Of course, I see your physical appearance with my eyes, but this does not mean much to me. Your physical appearance is just a fleeting image, like the images of a film that are projected onto a screen; it appears and disappears without leaving an impression. What I really want to see, or what I truly want to know, is the part of you that remains unchanged even with the passing of time as you live your ever-changing life. In other words, I would like to see your Buddha-nature. This is at the forefront of my mind when I interact with others.

2) Right Speech

Another important point of the Eightfold Path is Right Speech. This is difficult to practice but the easiest to identify for self-reflection. Speaking rightly is difficult. We cannot master this in just one or two years. Refining our words requires tremendous effort, but we must understand that human society is built on words.

Self-reflection on Right Speech is not only about the words you speak through your mouth but also about any expression of the thoughts in your mind. For example, it includes the words you write and your facial expression and body language, which may speak your mind more eloquently than your spoken words. Your face says more than your mouth. Your eyes speak, too. Each look in your eyes or expression on your face reveals your feelings toward others. Some people are only concerned with what they have said, but even if the spoken words were appropriate, what about your facial expression? What did your eyes say? This is what I would like you to think about. All body language is included in the self-reflection of Right Speech.

Ultimately, the Real World is a world of thoughts. In the Real World, thoughts and actions are not separate but are one and the same. Everything you think, be it good or bad, manifests immediately. In this world, however, your thoughts and the outcome are not directly linked. Your words and actions lie between them. Only with their intervention can your thoughts be manifested. Therefore, you must first be aware of the words you use.

Typical spirits in hell can be identified by the words they use; they never utter words to wish the happiness of others. Although they seem to be wishing for their own happiness, they do not realize that their words are clouding their divine nature.

Words are mysterious indeed; only a few things other than words can tell us more clearly whether we are living in accordance with God's Will. If practicing self-reflection is difficult for you, please think about the words you speak first. Try to imagine what the world of angels would be like. There is no heaven where people harm each other. In other words, heaven is created with words. The numerous spirits in hell have no physical body and exist as thought energy. If they want to change hell into heaven, they must correct their words. Then, a heavenly world will immediately begin to appear. It is that simple. However, hell is still full of people, which means many people are unable to practice the second path of the Eightfold Path.

Right Speech has no limits. This is also true for someone like me who is speaking to you. Ultimately, Right Speech must be filled with words of Truth, words that possess the strongest and most refined spiritual power. You cannot consider that you have completed self-reflection on Right Speech simply because you did not say harmful words to others. You need to examine how many words of Truth you were able to offer to others during the day. You must reach this level of self-reflection. There are many people who think their self-reflection is complete because they did not harm others with their words. But in fact, this is not the end of self-reflection. How many words of Truth did you convey to the people you met? Were you able to give nourishment to their souls and kindle a light in their hearts? Please know that this is how far your self-reflection must go.

3) Right Living

The Eightfold Path can be organized in many ways, but I would like to bring up Right Living next. I have explained it as living one's life rightly. The original meaning of Right

Living is to live life to the fullest. This means to manifest the original state of your soul that is now residing in your physical body at this time and in this space. This idea naturally leads us to live rightly. Accordingly, we need to reflect on our way of life every single day. Again, there is no completion to this self-reflection. Looking back on the last 24 hours of your day, there may be things you feel you have done well. Then, if you were asked, "Could you live these 24 hours more in accordance with God's Will? Is it possible for someone else who has more deeply awakened to the Truth to use those same hours more effectively?" What would you say? When you ask yourself these questions, you will realize that self-reflection on Right Living is never-ending.

In the context of modern life, Right Living would be the effective use of the time you have been given in this life. However, as I have written in *Starting from The Ordinary*, "time" here does not refer to relative time. Rather, it refers to absolute time. You are being evaluated by the time you spend living in absolute time within the 24 hours you have. Time has a different spiritual value for each one of us. Twenty-four hours can be measured with a clock, and every hour may seem to be the same for everyone. However, from the perspective of the Truth, one hour may not merely be one hour; an hour spent by one person may not be worth a minute or even a second for another, and that same hour can be worth a thousand or two thousand years to someone else. For those who listened to an hour of Jesus' sermon, the value of that one hour might have been equal to two thousand years in terms of absolute time. This does not refer to the amount of time you spend listening to lectures. It is the amount of time you spend in a day as your awakened self. This is what reflection on Right Living is. Many of you may think you have lived your day efficiently and effectively. However, when thinking about whether you were able to live each day as if it were your last or as if it were one or two thousand years, you will come to realize that there is infinite room for self-reflection on Right Living.

4) *Right Action*

The next path in the Eightfold Path is Right Action. For those who have a job, this path may seem similar to Right Living. But Right Action asks whether you have ever reflected on work itself. Most people live their lives without much thought; they think they just happen to be working at their company after graduating from school and will continue to work there until retirement; this is the norm in Japan.

Have you ever thought about how much of your time in life you spend working? Most people spend a third or more of their lifetime working upon entering society. Are you satisfied with using your time merely to earn a living? Are you working only to get paid? Isn't there valuable meaning in building relationships with people in your workplace? Suppose your life were to end today and you were to look back on your whole life. Wasn't there something you wanted to accomplish in your job? Isn't there a part of you who feels embarrassed for not exerting yourself to the fullest at work? Don't you feel sad for not having worked with all your heart and soul?

Your work is of great value in two respects. First, it is the starting point of building utopia. Societies and various environments change through work. Second, work provides us with materials to attain higher enlightenment. Work presents you with the opportunity to practice nurturing love of the Developmental Stages of Love. Without the working environment and the opportunities it presents, you cannot practice nurturing love. Therefore, we must appreciate the opportunity to raise our level of enlightenment through work; work serves as a place for us to deepen our enlightenment.

There are infinite ways to nurture people. For example, the development of even a company president, who has tens of thousands of employees to look after, through work is not limited to the number of employees within the company. He or she has the potential to go beyond their company and influence people on a national or even a global level. With regard to enlightenment, nurturing love has the potential to infinitely expand its influence. This limitless potential allows you to increase the strength of your soul and helps you become a person of greater caliber. Aside from the different spiritual levels of the soul, the soul has the capacity to embrace other people. Even a person who does not have a high level of enlightenment may have a great capacity for generosity and acceptance. Without practicing nurturing love on many different occasions, the capacity to embrace and guide many different people cannot be developed.

5) *Right Thought*

I have so far explained the first four paths of the Eightfold Path, which are very important for those pursuing spiritual discipline. However, for those seeking enlightenment and devoting themselves to self-discipline, Right Thought is crucial. Compared with the previously mentioned paths— Right View, Right Speech, Right Living, and Right Action, which are concrete practices that have a relatively easy starting point—Right Thought is difficult to practice, and many people cannot reach this stage. To what extent you are able to explore the path of Right Thought will tell you whether you are genuinely seeking enlightenment.

The mind is very interesting. At times, it appears to me like the images in a kaleidoscope; at other times, it appears like a bubble. The mind is ever-changing and can contract to a single point where the infinite expanse of the great universe lies. The ever-changing nature of the mind prompts us to realize that the true purpose of reincarnation throughout eternity is to fully understand Right Thought. We repeatedly reincarnate throughout eternity because this spiritual assignment of exploring Right Thought is never-ending.

I publish so many books on the Truth to provide material to help you pursue Right Thought. This material conveys Buddha's Truth. Unless you study this Truth, you will never truly understand Right Thought. The human mind is multi-faceted. But to us, it only appears as a two-dimensional structure, like a flat surface. To see the mind as a multi-faceted structure, studying the knowledge of Truth is essential, as it allows us to examine the world within our minds from every angle.

6) Right Effort

The path of Right Effort enhances and supports your practice of Right Thought, allowing you to make further progress. Right Effort means to make an effort on the right path or in the right direction. Although there is no hierarchy among human beings, if people were to be divided into two groups, one would be a group with those facing in the direction of God and the other would be a group with those facing the opposite direction. As a starting point, it is necessary to turn toward the direction of God. This is the first step toward happiness. This is your first step, direction, and aim. If you make a mistake here, your efforts will all be wasted no matter how hard you try. So face the right direction. Go forward on the right path one step at a time. This is Right Effort.

Here, I would like to clarify that the objective of Right Effort is to discover enlightenment. Without this goal, you could never say you are making Right Effort. Although the spiritual level of each person is different, and each of you lives in a different environment to pursue enlightenment, Right Effort is impossible without the aspiration to discover enlightenment.

To this end, strong will, courage, a sense of purpose, and energy are essential. Even if you are living your daily lives rightly, you must make sure you are not living like a plant.

Do you find yourself living each day without any ideals or a sense of purpose, like floating duckweeds on the surface of the water? Is that the right way to live? Put down strong roots and grow straight toward the sky, as if to push through to heaven. This is what Right Effort is all about. Please do not get this wrong. No matter how beautifully you may be drifting in a pure environment, like floating duckweeds on the clean water in an aquarium, this is absolutely not the true purpose of life. You must not just live through every day. Drifting in a pure environment is not the end. Right Effort is not just about the purity of the mind. Aim for something greater. Develop and grow like a giant tree. You must grow; if you do not, you cannot say you are a child of God. You cannot say you have Buddha-nature within.

7) Right Will

The last two paths of the Eightfold Path are Right Will and Right Meditation. These practices mark a spiritual discipline where you enter a professional level. After overcoming the hurdles of Right Will and Right Meditation, you will reach "the first stage of the awakened one" or become an "Arhat." At this level, a halo will appear around your head, and you will be able to receive messages from your guardian spirits.

You will also be able to give light to others. To reach this first stage of enlightenment, Right Will and Right Meditation are indispensable.

Right Will is not just about the thoughts and ideas that come and go every day. Instead, it is the direction of a will that is projected far into the future. In fact, the power of will in Right Will works like a locomotive engine that pulls Right Effort forward. The "will" here does not simply mean drawing up a plan for one's future; it includes the thoughts directed toward our guardian and guiding spirits, or what we call "prayer." Thoughts that arise and are transmitted with a specific purpose are what we call "will." Accordingly, Right Will in the Eightfold Path also includes prayers to God and to the high spirits close to God: prayers to correct yourself, prayers of gratitude—that is, to offer gratitude for the great blessings of having been given life—and prayers toward a wonderful future vision.

Numerous such thoughts are transmitted from our minds. Therefore, we can conclude: while we live in this three-dimensional world, we are also beings who transcend this third dimension. Depending on the soul, human beings are an existence that encompasses the multi-dimensional world within. Therefore, you must realize that Right Will is the way for us to transcend this third dimension by transmitting will in all directions and building a bridge from this world to the Real World. It is a way for us to move closer to God. For this reason, Right Will is there as a way to transcend this three-dimensional world while being in it.

8) Right Meditation

The final path is Right Meditation or meditating rightly. There are many kinds of meditation. For example, in self-reflective meditation, you clear the clouds covering your mind one by one. Right Meditation also includes the state of prayer—the state where you are constantly praying that connects you to the world of high spirits.

Through Right Meditation, we can experience emancipation while still living in this world. When we experience a spiritual state where we feel like our minds no longer belong to this three-dimensional world, we have completed Right Meditation. Only through this experience can we move beyond the restrictions of our physical bodies and three-dimensional materials and build our true selves as an existence of the higher dimensions. This is the goal of self-reflection that we must seek.

Self-reflection is a way to discover your true self as a child of God and to live in such a state in this world. I would like all of you to discover the wonderful self within you—the self that is connected to the higher dimensions. Self-reflection includes this kind of creative endeavor.

I have discussed the fundamental ideas of self-reflection from various perspectives. I conclude this lecture with an important message: without self-reflection, enlightenment is impossible.

CHAPTER FIVE

The Principle of
Prayer

The Fifth Public Lecture of 1988

Originally recorded in Japanese on December 18, 1988
at Tokyo Metropolitan Hibiya Public Hall in Tokyo, Japan
and later translated into English.

1

Building a Bridge to God

Finally, we come to the last principle, the Principle of Prayer. The previous lecture explored the Principle of Self-Reflection. The elements of prayer and self-reflection are essential when thinking about God. Those of you who have studied all the principles—starting with the Principle of Happiness, followed by the Principles of Love, the Mind, Enlightenment, Progress, Wisdom, Utopia, Salvation, and Self-Reflection—are probably beginning to understand the framework of my teachings. In this lecture, I would like to use the knowledge of Truth as a basis and teach the Principle of Prayer so that you can further understand the Truth and build a bridge to God.

No matter how much you study the Truth as knowledge, if you do not awaken to faith and have love for God, then 99 percent of your efforts will be fruitless. You are born into this three-dimensional world to have various experiences and acquire knowledge on a range of subjects. On many occasions in your life, you are given chances to awaken to the Truth. By passing through them, you are expected to come to a true understanding of Father God's Will and to live in tune with His will. There can be no compromise regarding this. We must not distort the Truth with mere academic studies and knowledge that humans have accumulated in the past. The Eternal Truth, the Everlasting Truth, the Immortal Truth continues to shine through the past, the present, and the future, piercing through hundreds of millions of years of time and space. I must grasp what remains unchanged within the flow of eternal time and reveal it to you. If I cannot do that, then my life this time would be meaningless. I want to grasp this unchanging Truth from the flow of eternal time and call on to the mind of each and every one of you at all costs. Unless I teach you this, I cannot fulfill my mission in this life. I would rather not have lived this life at all. Come what may, I am determined to convey the Truth God created in eternal time, the Will of God, the bursting energy of God, to each one of you. Otherwise, there is no point in having founded Happy Science, in having built its foundation, or in entering the age of expansion.

What did you expect to hear, learn, and see in my lectures? Some of you may purchase books of Truth, whereas others may seek the CDs and DVDs of my lectures. Why are you seeking the Truth? I certainly do not hold lectures and seminars simply for you to pass the time. I want people to realize the significance of the present times. The books in which the Truth is written are placed on shelves among countless other books, and determining how much the light and energy of these books differ from the others becomes difficult. That is why I give lectures and directly address people.

The lectures I give are mine but, at the same time, are not mine. This is Ryuho Okawa's lecture, but not Ryuho Okawa's lecture. Do you know where my words come from? Do you understand the origin of the vibration, the energy, and the light these words contain? Just as when Jesus spoke 2,000 years ago, this energy comes from the world of the greatest authority within the world you can perceive. You cannot directly experience this energy even after returning to the spirit world. The opportunity to experience this energy is being given to you now at this very moment. Words like these have not been heard for 2,000 years since Jesus Christ left this world. I dare say, now is the time when such words are being heard. These are not the words of a human being.

2

Be Pure in Heart

Self-reflection and prayer

What have you learned in the last lecture—the Principle of Self-Reflection? You probably learned to directly look at your inner self: to regain your true mind and to see God within this purity. Do you understand why this was taught to you? It is for you to remember the feelings you have already experienced long ago but have long since forgotten. The world of salvation does not exist in some faraway place that is completely separate from you; neither does the world of ideals nor the world of eternity. The ideal world or utopia that humankind has always sought exists in the very mind of each of you. This is what I wanted to convey in the lecture on self-reflection. Self-reflection aims to discover this Truth.

Once you find your true mind through self-reflection, you need to elevate your thoughts higher and higher. They must take off for a faraway world, the inner world, and after seeking the inner world, they must step out into the outer world, a world of flight, a multi-dimensional world, the original world, the primordial world, the world of genesis.

No matter how fervently I may wish to, I cannot communicate to you the feeling and experience of encountering higher dimensional consciousnesses and the world to which they belong. The world of higher dimensions is beyond description. Once you witness its majesty and its beauty filled with power, your understanding of the significance of this earthly world will completely change. Awakening to that world means you are stepping into a world where humans are both human and not human—a world that is in this earthly world and is not in this earthly world. Prayer is the way to get there.

Prayer has some difficult aspects. When our minds are surrounded by third dimensional vibrations, our prayers tend to become distorted and, at times, reach completely unexpected worlds. As someone who teaches prayer, I must strictly remind you of this. This is what the angels in the other world are always hoping for. At times, your prayers do not reach heaven no matter how much you pray. You may wonder "why?" An undeniable fact is that a certain set of rules governs the world of prayer. We must accept this fact and learn these rules.

The rules of prayer

What are the rules of prayer? First, be pure in heart. I usually recommend first practicing self-reflection, then meditation, and then prayer, but when you directly start from prayer, you must first be pure in heart. Unless this first step is fulfilled, your prayers will not reach heaven because the world that receives prayers is a purehearted world.

Prayer is like a telephone call; it is the act of connecting lines of "thought." It is also the act of directing your mind toward the heavenly world. Therefore, prayer has certain requirements, the first being purity of heart. Because the world beyond this one is a world of thoughts, for your prayers to attune to that world, you, yourself, need to send out thoughts that correspond to that world. In Buddhist teachings, being purehearted is often expressed as "removing attachment." But in this lecture, "The Principle of Prayer," I will simply say, "Be pure in heart."

You probably meet various people every day. How often do you meet a purehearted person? How often do you find someone who impresses you with their purity of heart? When you look at yourself, to what extent can you confidently declare you have been living with a pure heart? No matter how earnestly you may be trying to live your life with a pure heart, it is only natural for your mind to become entangled in various thoughts in the process of living and change the direction it faces.

To more clearly explain "purity of heart," I would say purity of heart allows you to experience moments of transparency in which you feel the self has disappeared. When you reflect on your day, do you find yourself filling your 24-hour-long day with thoughts focusing entirely on yourself? Do your thoughts throughout the day consist entirely of concerns about your own happiness or unhappiness? Can you discover a time of purity when you remove the word "I" from your mind? Are you able to have thoughts that do not have the subject "I"? Can you rejoice for joy? To enter the world of prayer, subjects such as "I" and "he" or "human" and "God" become unnecessary. The only requirement is that you become one with the energy that flows throughout the entire universe.

To this end, be infinitely transparent.

Radiate the beautiful brilliance in such a state.

That is what is important.

Rather than feeling the love for yourself,

Feel the love for love.

Rather than savoring the love for others,

Savor the love for love.

Love it because it is love.

Love it because it is joy.

Savor this love.

Savor the joy that joy is joy.

Put these words into practice.

Rather than praying for something or someone,

Discover prayer in prayer.

Find prayer in prayer.

Enjoy the purity within you

That exists because of your pure heart.

Savor this purity.

Appreciate it not for yourself

Or for anyone else,

But simply for itself.

Experiencing oneness with God

When you reach this state, your mind will be transparent: your thoughts will be purified, and those thoughts will no longer need an object or target. The "what" and "who" will vanish, and your prayers will become pure. Then, at this moment, you will experience a state of oneness with God. This very moment is the greatest possible moment of happiness a human being can be blessed with. In Buddhist terms, it is called "Great Enlightenment." Another way to put it is "oneness with God." In this state, there is no distinction between the Will of God and the will of the self. Ideally, we should constantly maintain this state, but as ordinary human beings, we may find this task difficult; Therefore, I suggest taking at least a few moments every day to experience oneness with God.

As for myself, I am extremely grateful to be able to live in a state of oneness with God 24 hours a day. This is possible because I have no desire to live my life for myself. I want to use my life for God in any way I can. Based on outward appearances, it is true that I may need to spend my time to live for myself as a human being. But on the inside, I have no intention of living for myself. To serve as the foundation for something greater, I sublimate myself and become selfless and transparent.

A trait of those who live their days in a state of total oneness with God is that they no longer have personal worries. You probably have your own unique concerns, which you believe to be different from the difficulties of others. However, having worries indicates you have not yet attained a state of oneness with God. The greater, the deeper, and the more diverse your suffering is, the further you are from becoming one with God; your suffering indicates you are becoming smaller and smaller and are still living within the world of trial and error.

3

The Meaning of True Prayer

A passion to bring happiness to all humankind

To experience true prayer—to actually experience oneness with God—you must first get rid of the troublesome impediments of everyday worries and distress. Unless you solve these problems, your mind cannot attune to God's Will. Then, what will you do? I can almost hear your inner voice saying, "But I've never met anyone who doesn't have worries." You may be saying this to justify yourself and thinking it is only natural to be one of those "ever suffering people."

However, I would suggest the reverse. You are allowed to worry if you want to. But consider the nature of your worries. Make them of a higher quality. What are you worrying about? Ask yourself if your worries are the kind that you would not mind telling others about. You may be exaggerating trifling concerns that are not really worth spending time on. If you are going to worry, do it seriously and on behalf of God. Worry about something more important. Worry about people other than yourself. Once you begin to worry on behalf of God, you will understand the true nature of the worries that have been weighing on your mind. You may be worrying about something as small as a poppy seed. In truth, you should have more important things to worry about, but because you are unaware of what you should be worrying about, you magnify trivial concerns as your mind sways in a state of confusion.

If you are going to worry about something, worry about the same thing as God, assuming He has worries, that is. If God has any worries at all, these would not be called "worries" but rather "passion"—a passion to improve the world and to bring light and happiness into it. Transform your worries into this kind of "passion." When you take another look at your inner world from the grand perspective of passion, you will feel the parasites known as "worries" that were possessing you dropping away one after another. You suffering from worries is an indication that you have not yet awakened to a great mission—a great passion.

People cannot think of two things at once. This is a truth and a psychological law. Therefore, change what is in your mind; fill your mind with something entirely different—with the passion to bring happiness to all people. This is the best way to become free of worries. Anyone who is struggling by him or herself in loneliness, with a frown on his or her face, can experience a sudden transformation and begin to radiate a brilliant light. I would like everyone to experience that moment. Awakening to this moment is the first step to great prayer.

Angels are standing beyond the gate of prayer

If you are thinking about learning the Principle of Prayer in an attempt to gain something, please abandon that thought. Remove it from your mind. Cast it out completely. Such thoughts have already closed the gateway to prayer, the gateway to oneness with the Great One. To become one with the Great One and to enter the royal road to life's success, discarding all that is unnecessary or trivial is essential. Those who wish to learn how to pray to achieve some small ambitions cannot pass through the gateway of prayer. Such people are not permitted to even stand in front of the gate.

Large numbers of angels are in fact standing just beyond the gate of prayer; here lies the difference between prayer and the other rules of enlightenment. The moment you pass through the gate, you will have to face the angels. How, in your current state of mind, can you face numerous angels? Are you not ashamed to show yourself and reveal your thoughts before so many angels? Words like self-reflection and even repentance cannot sufficiently describe this feeling of shame. After some years or decades, each one of you without exception will leave your physical body and return to the heavenly world. At that time, you will stand before the angels. Have you ever thought about how you might feel when you stand in front of them? At that moment, without anyone pointing it out to you, you will realize how trivial and unimportant the desires you sought in your thoughts and actions have been. You will realize you should not be allowed to stand before the angels as you are; their presence will be too dazzling. Their light is the kind that makes you feel as if you are disappearing—as if you are fading away. Faced with this dazzling light, you can no longer think or hold on to any desires. You will certainly experience this as a reality sooner or later.

To pray means to experience at this very moment, today, what you will actually experience at some time in the future, be it years or decades from now. In other words, entering the world of prayer means you are already dead. The physical body you reside in is as good as dead. I hope you understand me. At that moment, you are a "dead person" in the three-dimensional world. However, seen from the worlds of the fourth dimension and beyond, you are a "living person." Those of you who have read my books probably already understand this. In this world, death is perceived as misfortune or something that brings grief and agony, but from the perspective of the inhabitants of the Real World, "life" in this world is indeed "death" itself.

Perhaps "death" is too strong a word, but it is at least true that people living in this world grope around blindly— unable to see the Truth, unable to act as they truly want, and unable to understand God's Will or the will of their guardian and guiding spirits. As they blindly fumble, they mistakenly believe they are enjoying the freedom to the fullest. However, from the perspective of the Real World, this life is not freedom at all; it is merely a state where people are crawling around trying to grasp at whatever their hands can touch in an environment where they can neither see nor hear anything. Nevertheless, they consider this state as "freedom" or "respect for individual character." From a political perspective, they consider this "democracy." But this is a grave mistake. Freedom is nothing like this. You might have seen just how little freedom a newborn baby has, but from the perspective of the spiritual world, every single adult in this world is just like these infants. In moments of self-reflection or moments of prayer, which is a deeper state than self-reflection, we who seem to be no different from "babies" or even seem to be "dead" leave this world for an instant or for some time to return to the world we originally came from. These are the moments when we are truly free— when we return to our original state of freedom.

Being reborn through prayer

Viewed from the earthly world, prayer can be considered a bridge to God and the high spirits; however, from the perspective of the Real World, prayer is an act of gaining life. It is an act of awakening to eternal life once again; it is the moment when we reveal our true selves to the Sun of the Truth. For those living in this world, the moment of prayer is like the moment of "death." It is death but also rebirth; through prayer, we are reborn. If we are reborn through prayer, we can no longer continue to live as the same person we were before. If, after prayer, we continue to live and think in the same way we had been before, what was the point of dying and coming back to life? If the act of prayer is like reincarnation experienced in a "moment," then why wouldn't we change within that moment?

Prayer is a reincarnation that occurs in the world of the mind. It is the effort to transform the self. Prayers recited in an attempt to merely benefit oneself or to get a windfall are not true prayers. Such prayers have been offered time and again for hundreds and thousands of years but have always been rejected in the name of Truth. True prayer is a rebirth. The moment we get a glimpse of the Real World, we cannot help but be born anew. Only by being reborn in this way can one experience rebirth in this lifetime. For this reason, I repeatedly say that the moment you pray to God, your past will be completely cut off from your present life. If you have not been transformed by praying, you must think about what would happen to that prayer. You must understand that it could very well turn into a sword that attacks you. When a person, despite having an awareness of the existence of the Real World, recites a prayer that is not accompanied by transformation, the prayer can turn into a sword that slashes at eternal life. This is what happens to people who use prayers for selfish purposes.

4

Filling Your Heart with Love for God

What happens to misguided prayers?

Prayer works according to the laws of energy. Therefore, any wish that takes the form of prayer will be heard by someone, even if it does not reach God. It may be heard by the inhabitants of hell, who also listen to the thoughts and wishes of those in this world. Sometimes, they give people a "helping hand" as part of their own brand of kindness. Those who receive help from such beings will gradually be captivated by them and therefore contribute to the expansion of hellish thought energy. This is why I need to clearly explain how misguided prayers can be a source of energy for the inhabitants of hell.

Hell is an indescribably miserable world, but even the spirits in hell abide by the laws of energy. In hell, dense clouds of negative thoughts block the light of the Spiritual Sun. Then, how do the spirits live under such conditions? The spirits in heaven directly receive energy from the Spiritual Sun, but the spirits in hell cannot. Therefore, they use the negative thoughts generated by the people in this world as a source of energy for their activities. Most of these thoughts contain selfish objectives, and these bad desires end up in hell.

You might laugh off these facts about evil spirits and devils as a joke. Even if you acknowledge their existence, you might think it has nothing to do with you. However, such evil spirits and devils remain active using the energy generated by the negative thoughts, or wrong and self-cherishing thoughts, of each and every person.

Therefore, you must pursue prayer, seek God, and fill your heart with love for God as seriously as if you are standing on a cliff of a mountain or at a crossroads of life and death. Praying without such a mindset will result in a completely opposite effect. What will happen to your prayers that turn into energy for the spirits in hell? This energy enlarges them, makes them more active, and turns into the power used to drag people in this world toward the wrong direction. This is a vicious cycle. Once you become aware of this cycle, you must end it at all costs. It must not be allowed to continue.

The resolution to be reborn

Saying that we must get rid of hell is easy. Perhaps some people question why God and the high spirits do not eliminate it altogether. However, given the current circumstances, hell cannot be eliminated without destroying this earthly world. In this case, would you choose to dissolve this earthly world to get rid of hell? What does it mean to eliminate this world? It means to totally eradicate all hope for prosperity, development, and progress that God had in the beginning.

What would you do when this world, which was originally created for the progress and development of humankind, pursues the opposite goal and becomes a supply source of evil and a stronghold of evil? Would you destroy it, or would you allow it to continue existing? If it were destroyed, evil would disappear. But what would remain after the evil is eliminated? There would be stagnation, depletion, and extinction—a world without prosperity or progress. Would we be satisfied with such a world? No, we certainly would not.

Presuming we allow this world to continue to exist, what would we need to do? The answer is clear. Because hell is created in the Real World by the negative thoughts caused by life in the earthly world, we must rid this world of negative thoughts through our own efforts. The only way to purify the earth as we aim for progress and development is to undergo a complete turnaround in mindset and attune our will closer to God's Will. What other ways do we have? That is why many people need to stop living the way they have been living, once and for all. Please make a clean break with your past today and begin a new life tomorrow. So, today is a day for you to pray for that.

I would like you to pray to God: "I will make a break with my past and make a new start. Please allow me to become someone who can live in tune with God's Will." Please pray with the resolve that you will definitely change. If you have made many mistakes in the past and have troubled other people, both alive and dead, you must first repent for those mistakes. Then, be reborn and start afresh. This resolution to be reborn will, in itself, turn into divine power from the outside and will save you. Where there is determination, there is light from other-power.

5

Self-Power and Other-Power

The two major paths to spiritual discipline are "self-power" and "other power." It is not uncommon for people to think of these paths as completely different. "Self-power" is the idea of discovering or encountering God or Buddha as you refine yourself, whereas "other-power" is the idea of abandoning such thought of self-effort and obeying God to attain enlightenment followed by happiness.

However, the Truth is not exclusively in either path. It runs through both. Each of these paths appears to be close to the Truth yet far from it. Each seems far away from the Truth yet close to it. They appear to be two separate paths, yet they are not. In other words, those who do not intend to truly change themselves for the better will not be blessed with the grace of other-power. There is essentially no distinction between being saved through self-power and being saved through other-power. They are two different names for the same doorway leading to oneness with God. Once you know that God's blessings and grace are not given to those who do not try to change themselves at the root, you will understand that the conventional idea of being saved through other-power disappears. It is an idea that must disappear.

Even if the teachings were true at first, people have a tendency to distort these teachings in a way that is convenient for themselves as they pass down the teachings. People have such a weakness, a shallow level of understanding. Even if you think you understand the teachings now, as time passes and in the process of conveying them to others, they tend to change owing to a lack of understanding and self-cherishing thoughts. These are the two main causes of division among religions and the resulting religious conflicts both in the past and present. Before directly encountering God through prayer, we need to check ourselves and see if there is any danger of yielding to either of them. We must ensure that our understanding of the teachings is correct and that we are not using the Truth for our own convenience. When these two dangers are truly understood, the causes of religious conflicts will be completely eliminated. These two weaknesses were and are, and possibly will be, the source of every conflict.

What will save us from these two traps? The first solution is to have infinite enthusiasm for exploring the Truth or the attitude of trying to explore the Truth through and through. Never forget this. Do not force the Truth you found onto others as if it is the only Truth. Continue to seek the Truth thoroughly.

The second solution is to experience the truly overwhelming energy of the world of the absolute or the

Diamond Realm in the Real World. Experiencing this will naturally lead to humility. People have created a stronghold or castle called "modern civilization" with their minds; they lock themselves up there and behave as supreme rulers. However, as soon as they understand the tremendous power of the true world, this castle hopelessly collapses. No matter how wise a person living in this world may be, that person's knowledge does not amount to even one-billionth or one-trillionth of God's Wisdom. People often misunderstand this. Human abilities are very limited and insignificant, yet people tend to be deluded by earthly titles, positions, and reputations. Those who have glimpsed the awesome world of Truth have no choice but to be truly humble. If you still feel you have a tendency to be too proud of yourself or become conceited quite easily, this indicates you have not yet come in contact with the world of Truth or really experienced its overwhelming energy. The more you know and understand the world of Truth, the smaller you will see yourself to be.

6

Three Conditions for Prayer

The first condition—beauty

Once you perceive that you are no bigger than a bean, you will be able to see God with a mind that is pure, clear, and transparent. When you pray in this state, you will begin to give out a brilliant light, just like a star shining in the sky. This brilliance has a mystical glow and an infinitely profound radiance to it: therein lies a form of beauty.

Beauty is what makes faith true faith and prayer true prayer. Beauty is what proves that your faith and your prayer are real. If you pray in a selfish way, will you appear beautiful? If you pray in self-preservation, will you appear beautiful in the eyes of an objective observer? If you were to view your prayers from the position of a "bona fide third party," would you appear beautiful? Look very carefully. Selfish prayers born of greed are never beautiful. But prayers that really receive the Light of God are divine and beautiful. For this reason, I would like to present "beauty" as the standard for checking your prayers objectively.

If you want to check whether you are praying in the right way, look at yourself praying and see if you appear beautiful. Look squarely at yourself, the contents of your prayer, the words you are using, your attitude, and your facial expression, as if you were looking at yourself in a mirror. Is there beauty? If you find any ugliness, put down the mirror and stop praying. Stop standing before the gate of prayer. You must realize you are not ready to pray and are not in a position to pray.

The second condition—goodness

I have highlighted "beauty" as a condition of true prayer, and you may be wondering if there are any other conditions. Yes, there certainly are. Beauty alone is not enough. Beautiful prayer must have "goodness" within. So ask yourself again whether your prayers are oriented toward goodness. For them to be truly good, your prayers must not be embarrassing to write down for others to read. In fact, just having other people read it is not enough. You must be comfortable sharing the content of your prayers with your guardian and guiding spirits, high spirits, or God. Is your prayer good or not? A prayer that is not good is accompanied by shame.

Everyone has the feeling of shame within, but many people may not be aware of the reason for its existence. Shame exists as a standard by which to judge what is good. When the mind moves away from goodness, a sense of shame naturally arises in your conscience. This sense of shame is accompanied by a feeling of not wanting to be seen by others. In other words, the fact that we have a sense of shame itself is proof that our minds were created to pursue goodness. The feeling of shame is given to each one of us so that we can check ourselves when we deviate from goodness.

Although God has given human beings freedom of thought, He strongly wishes us to choose goodness. This is why the feeling of shame arises when we choose something other than goodness. Please be aware of how ingeniously the human mind has been designed. When you trust the gauge of goodness that is embedded within you, you will naturally know what you should pray for.

The third condition—love

So far, I said prayer must contain beauty and goodness. Nevertheless, another condition for prayer is that it must always be accompanied by "love." A prayer without love is not a prayer: it is just dead words. This is my conclusion because those who do not have love do not know God. Those who do not know God cannot truly pray. One cannot understand God through knowledge alone. Love is essential in knowing God. Within love is a way to find God. Therefore, the infinite path of prayer is also the infinite path of love. The act of praying exists in the first place for the purpose of realizing great love.

The power of a human being confined in this three-dimensional physical body is limited, far from infinite. Prayer allows this limited power to develop and become infinite. This applies to myself as well. To make this power infinite, we need prayer. After all, true prayer is for the sake of love. It comes from the love for many others. Prayer is your desire to contribute your work and your efforts to benefit many others. Prayer is your wish to make the most of your life for the sake of many, including those who will be born in the future.

To me, prayer is the same as love. Love is prayer and prayer is love because God Himself is love. Nothing else but love can connect and unite God to me and me to God. Love is the word and concept that ties God and human beings. If you cannot understand love, you cannot truly pray.

Then, what is love? What makes love true? You need to understand love more deeply. Love is infinitely good. Love is infinitely wonderful. Love is infinite joy and infinite enlightenment. To understand love also means to attain enlightenment. Once you understand love and have established a pathway of love within you, through this pathway, you will be able to see and understand all the worlds God created; this is called "enlightenment." The joy of understanding, or "enlightenment," leads into the next step: the development of love. Understanding leads to enlightenment and enlightenment leads to the development of love. I would like you to understand that enlightenment is the driving force behind the development of love.

In summary, I have presented the three conditions of prayer. I am not certain whether you can fully understand them right now, but at the very least, I would like you to know that prayer must be accompanied by beauty, goodness, and love as a basic premise. Prayer without these three conditions is not true prayer.

7

The Power of Prayer

A prayer that fulfills these conditions will exert extraordinary power. In a sense, prayer has the greatest power of all, for it transcends human power. I presume not many people have witnessed the angels in the heavenly world responding to prayer, but high spirits possess tremendous power, indeed. If I pray for the creation of utopia, that prayer will resonate among thousands or tens of thousands of angels, and they will respond to my prayer.

What happens after they respond? Those in this world and those in heaven will unite to begin various activities to develop and create a wonderful world together. The fruit of prayer is the awakening and arousing of a supreme force— other-power. Once this power is involved, you will be able to go beyond the limits of your physical existence and transcend as human beings.

I would like to conclude this lecture with a prayer to God.

Prayer for Creating Utopia

O Great God,
We sincerely thank you
For giving us this opportunity.
With this opportunity,
May your Love fill the earth,
May your Light fill heaven,
May your Glory fill the entire world.
O God, please give us strength,
Give us infinite power,
And give us the courage to create Utopia.
May we be able to work in accordance with your Will
For the sake of a great ideal,
For the sake of a great creation,
For the sake of a wonderful new world,
For the sake of a new era,
For the sake of young people
Who will come after us,
And for the sake of the future people of this country
And future people of the world.
May this movement of love which we have launched,
This movement to bring happiness to all humankind,
Continue to shine brightly
Far into the future.
O God, we truly thank you.

Afterword to The Principle of Enlightenment

The principle of enlightenment, the principle of progress, and the principle of wisdom, which play pivotal roles in the Laws, are taught in this book. These principles are the compass of the mind, so if you are undergoing spiritual training based on the Truth, you cannot live without them. Being strict with yourself and being steady prevents souls from falling as they advance, while also maintaining harmony with other people.

In particular, the idea of progress through the Middle Way and the developmental stages of wisdom will promise the eternal advancement of your soul.

Ryuho Okawa
Master & CEO of Happy Science Group
October 1990

Afterword to The Principle of Utopia

I have compiled the Principle of Utopia, the Principle of Salvation, the Principle of Self-Reflection, and the Principle of Prayer—the last of my principles series—into one book. The Principle of Self-Reflection, in particular, is filled with power; based on its content, it can be considered a sequel to the Principle of Enlightenment. I highly recommend those who are troubled by negative spiritual influences to carefully read and study this principle and to repeatedly listen to the recording of this lecture. This lecture has the power to repel any devils no matter how strong they may be. It is endowed with the spiritual power of Buddha to drive away any evil spirits.

May this book find its way to all people. The daybreak for humankind is near. I believe so.

Ryuho Okawa
Master & CEO of Happy Science Group
October 1990

Afterword to the newly revised second volume of
The Ten Principles from El Cantare

After reading *The Ten Principles from El Cantare Volume I* and *Volume II*, exactly "who" I am may have become clear to many. My teachings are far beyond what a human being can teach.

These Laws were taught 32 years ago and are still applicable today.

On July 15, 1991, the Celebration of Lord El Cantare's Descent was held in Tokyo Dome. A young journalist from *Financial Times* covered this event and wrote a full-page article stating, "He is beyond Jesus Christ" and "Japan bows to a new god." Twenty-five years later, this journalist has become the head of an American media group. He attended my English lecture in New York, where he heard the prophecy of Donald Trump becoming the new president one month prior to the election.

The Ten Principles from El Cantare is already part of human history. It is my mission to reprint this book with as little editing as possible.

Ryuho Okawa
Master & CEO of Happy Science Group
August 9, 2020

THE TEN PRINCIPLES FROM EL CANTARE VOLUME I

Ryuho Okawa's First Lectures on His Basic Teachings

CHAPTER ONE   The Principle of Happiness

CHAPTER TWO   The Principle of Love

CHAPTER THREE The Principle of the Mind

CHAPTER FOUR   The Principle of Enlightenment

CHAPTER FIVE   The Principle of Progress

Paperback • 232 pages • $16.95
ISBN: 978-1-942125-85-3 (Dec. 6, 2021)

ABOUT THE AUTHOR

RYUHO OKAWA was born on July 7th 1956, in Tokushima, Japan. After graduating from the University of Tokyo with a law degree, he joined a Tokyo-based trading house. While working at its New York headquarters, he studied international finance at the Graduate Center of the City University of New York. In 1981, he attained Great Enlightenment and became aware that he is El Cantare with a mission to bring salvation to all humankind. In 1986, he established Happy Science. It now has members in over 160 countries across the world, with more than 700 branches and temples as well as 10,000 missionary houses around the world. The total number of lectures has exceeded 3,400 (of which more than 150 are in English) and over 2,950 books (of which more than 600 are Spiritual Interview Series) have been published, many of which are translated into 37 languages. Many of the books, including *The Laws of the Sun* have become best sellers or million sellers. To date, Happy Science has produced 24 movies. The original story and original concept were given by the Executive Producer Ryuho Okawa. Recent movie titles are *Into the Dreams...and Horror Experiences* (live-action, August 2021), *The Laws of the Universe - The Age of Elohim* (animation movie, October 2021), *The Cherry Bushido* (live-action, February 2022). He has also composed the lyrics and music of over 450 songs, such as theme songs and featured songs of movies. Moreover, he is the Founder of Happy Science University and Happy Science Academy (Junior and Senior High School), Founder and President of the Happiness Realization Party, Founder and Honorary Headmaster of Happy Science Institute of Government and Management, Founder of IRH Press Co., Ltd., and the Chairperson of NEW STAR PRODUCTION Co., Ltd. and ARI Production Co., Ltd.

WHAT IS EL CANTARE?

El Cantare means "the Light of the Earth," and is the Supreme God of the Earth who has been guiding humankind since the beginning of Genesis. He is whom Jesus called Father and Muhammad called Allah, and is *Ame-no-Mioya-Gami*, Japanese Father God. Different parts of El Cantare's core consciousness have descended to Earth in the past, once as Alpha and another as Elohim. His branch spirits, such as Shakyamuni Buddha and Hermes, have descended to Earth many times and helped to flourish many civilizations. To unite various religions and to integrate various fields of study in order to build a new civilization on Earth, a part of the core consciousness has descended to Earth as Master Ryuho Okawa.

Alpha is a part of the core consciousness of El Cantare who descended to Earth around 330 million years ago. Alpha preached Earth's Truths to harmonize and unify Earth-born humans and space people who came from other planets.

Elohim is a part of El Cantare's core consciousness who descended to Earth around 150 million years ago. He gave wisdom, mainly on the differences of light and darkness, good and evil.

Ame-no-Mioya-Gami (Japanese Father God) is the Creator God and the Father God who appears in the ancient literature, *Hotsuma Tsutae*. It is believed that He descended on the foothills of Mt. Fuji about 30,000 years ago and built the Fuji dynasty, which is the root of the Japanese civilization. With justice as the central pillar, Ame-no-Mioya-Gami's teachings spread to ancient civilizations of other countries in the world.

Shakyamuni Buddha was born as a prince into the Shakya Clan in India around 2,600 years ago. When he was 29 years old, he renounced the world and sought enlightenment. He later attained Great Enlightenment and founded Buddhism.

Hermes is one of the 12 Olympian gods in Greek mythology, but the spiritual Truth is that he taught the teachings of love and progress around 4,300 years ago that became the origin of the current Western civilization. He is a hero that truly existed.

Ophealis was born in Greece around 6,500 years ago and was the leader who took an expedition to as far as Egypt. He is the God of miracles, prosperity, and arts, and is known as Osiris in the Egyptian mythology.

Rient Arl Croud was born as a king of the ancient Incan Empire around 7,000 years ago and taught about the mysteries of the mind. In the heavenly world, he is responsible for the interactions that take place between various planets.

Thoth was an almighty leader who built the golden age of the Atlantic civilization around 12,000 years ago. In the Egyptian mythology, he is known as god Thoth.

Ra Mu was a leader who built the golden age of the civilization of Mu around 17,000 years ago. As a religious leader and a politician, he ruled by uniting religion and politics.

ABOUT HAPPY SCIENCE

Happy Science is a global movement that empowers individuals to find purpose and spiritual happiness and to share that happiness with their families, societies, and the world. With more than 12 million members around the world, Happy Science aims to increase awareness of spiritual truths and expand our capacity for love, compassion, and joy so that together we can create the kind of world we all wish to live in.

Activities at Happy Science are based on the Principle of Happiness (Love, Wisdom, Self-Reflection, and Progress). This principle embraces worldwide philosophies and beliefs, transcending boundaries of culture and religions.

Love teaches us to give ourselves freely without expecting anything in return; it encompasses giving, nurturing, and forgiving.

Wisdom leads us to the insights of spiritual truths, and opens us to the true meaning of life and the will of God (the universe, the highest power, Buddha).

Self-Reflection brings a mindful, nonjudgmental lens to our thoughts and actions to help us find our truest selves—the essence of our souls—and deepen our connection to the highest power. It helps us attain a clean and peaceful mind and leads us to the right life path.

Progress emphasizes the positive, dynamic aspects of our spiritual growth—actions we can take to manifest and spread happiness around the world. It's a path that not only expands our soul growth, but also furthers the collective potential of the world we live in.

PROGRAMS AND EVENTS

The doors of Happy Science are open to all. We offer a variety of programs and events, including self-exploration and self-growth programs, spiritual seminars, meditation and contemplation sessions, study groups, and book events.

Our programs are designed to:
* Deepen your understanding of your purpose and meaning in life
* Improve your relationships and increase your capacity to love unconditionally
* Attain peace of mind, decrease anxiety and stress, and feel positive
* Gain deeper insights and a broader perspective on the world
* Learn how to overcome life's challenges
  ... and much more.

For more information, visit <u>happy-science.org</u>.

CONTACT INFORMATION

Happy Science is a worldwide organization with branches and temples around the globe. For a comprehensive list, visit the worldwide directory at *happy-science.org*. The following are some of the many Happy Science locations:

UNITED STATES AND CANADA

New York
79 Franklin St., New York, NY 10013, USA
Phone: 1-212-343-7972
Fax: 1-212-343-7973
Email: ny@happy-science.org
Website: happyscience-usa.org

New Jersey
66 Hudson St., #2R, Hoboken, NJ 07030, USA
Phone: 1-201-313-0127
Email: nj@happy-science.org
Website: happyscience-usa.org

Chicago
2300 Barrington Rd., Suite #400, Hoffman Estates, IL 60169, USA
Phone: 1-630-937-3077
Email: chicago@happy-science.org
Website: happyscience-usa.org

Florida
5208 8th St., Zephyrhills, FL 33542, USA
Phone: 1-813-715-0000
Fax: 1-813-715-0010
Email: florida@happy-science.org
Website: happyscience-usa.org

Atlanta
1874 Piedmont Ave., NE Suite 360-C
Atlanta, GA 30324, USA
Phone: 1-404-892-7770
Email: atlanta@happy-science.org
Website: happyscience-usa.org

San Francisco
525 Clinton St.
Redwood City, CA 94062, USA
Phone & Fax: 1-650-363-2777
Email: sf@happy-science.org
Website: happyscience-usa.org

Los Angeles
1590 E. Del Mar Blvd., Pasadena, CA 91106, USA
Phone: 1-626-395-7775
Fax: 1-626-395-7776
Email: la@happy-science.org
Website: happyscience-usa.org

Orange County
16541 Gothard St. Suite 104
Huntington Beach, CA 92647
Phone: 1-714-659-1501
Email: oc@happy-science.org
Website: happyscience-usa.org

San Diego
7841 Balboa Ave. Suite #202
San Diego, CA 92111, USA
Phone: 1-626-395-7775
Fax: 1-626-395-7776
E-mail: sandiego@happy-science.org
Website: happyscience-usa.org

Hawaii
Phone: 1-808-591-9772
Fax: 1-808-591-9776
Email: hi@happy-science.org
Website: happyscience-usa.org

Kauai
3343 Kanakolu Street, Suite 5
Lihue, HI 96766, USA
Phone: 1-808-822-7007
Fax: 1-808-822-6007
Email: kauai-hi@happy-science.org
Website: happyscience-usa.org

Toronto
845 The Queensway
Etobicoke, ON M8Z 1N6, Canada
Phone: 1-416-901-3747
Email: toronto@happy-science.org
Website: happy-science.ca

Vancouver
#201-2607 East 49th Avenue,
Vancouver, BC, V5S 1J9, Canada
Phone: 1-604-437-7735
Fax: 1-604-437-7764
Email: vancouver@happy-science.org
Website: happy-science.ca

INTERNATIONAL

Tokyo
1-6-7 Togoshi, Shinagawa,
Tokyo, 142-0041, Japan
Phone: 81-3-6384-5770
Fax: 81-3-6384-5776
Email: tokyo@happy-science.org
Website: happy-science.org

Seoul
74, Sadang-ro 27-gil,
Dongjak-gu, Seoul, Korea
Phone: 82-2-3478-8777
Fax: 82-2-3478-9777
Email: korea@happy-science.org
Website: happyscience-korea.org

London
3 Margaret St.
London, W1W 8RE United Kingdom
Phone: 44-20-7323-9255
Fax: 44-20-7323-9344
Email: eu@happy-science.org
Website: www.happyscience-uk.org

Taipei
No. 89, Lane 155, Dunhua N. Road,
Songshan District, Taipei City 105, Taiwan
Phone: 886-2-2719-9377
Fax: 886-2-2719-5570
Email: taiwan@happy-science.org
Website: happyscience-tw.org

Sydney
516 Pacific Highway, Lane Cove North,
2066 NSW, Australia
Phone: 61-2-9411-2877
Fax: 61-2-9411-2822
Email: sydney@happy-science.org

Kuala Lumpur
No 22A, Block 2, Jalil Link Jalan Jalil Jaya
2, Bukit Jalil 57000,
Kuala Lumpur, Malaysia
Phone: 60-3-8998-7877
Fax: 60-3-8998-7977
Email: malaysia@happy-science.org
Website: happyscience.org.my

Sao Paulo
Rua. Domingos de Morais 1154,
Vila Mariana, Sao Paulo SP
CEP 04010-100, Brazil
Phone: 55-11-5088-3800
Email: sp@happy-science.org
Website: happyscience.com.br

Kathmandu
Kathmandu Metropolitan City,
Ward No. 15, Ring Road, Kimdol,
Sitapaila Kathmandu, Nepal
Phone: 977-1-427-2931
Email: nepal@happy-science.org

Jundiai
Rua Congo, 447, Jd. Bonfiglioli
Jundiai-CEP, 13207-340, Brazil
Phone: 55-11-4587-5952
Email: jundiai@happy-science.org

Kampala
Plot 877 Rubaga Road, Kampala
P.O. Box 34130 Kampala, UGANDA
Phone: 256-79-4682-121
Email: uganda@happy-science.org

The Happiness Realization Party (HRP) was founded in May 2009 by Master Ryuho Okawa as part of the Happy Science Group. HRP strives to improve the Japanese society, based on three basic political principles of "freedom, democracy, and faith," and let Japan promote individual and public happiness from Asia to the world as a leader nation.

1) Diplomacy and Security: Protecting Freedom, Democracy, and Faith of Japan and the World from China's Totalitarianism

Japan's current defense system is insufficient against China's expanding hegemony and the threat of North Korea's nuclear missiles. Japan, as the leader of Asia, must strengthen its defense power and promote strategic diplomacy together with the nations which share the values of freedom, democracy, and faith. Further, HRP aims to realize world peace under the leadership of Japan, the nation with the spirit of religious tolerance.

2) Economy: Early economic recovery through utilizing the "wisdom of the private sector"

Economy has been damaged severely by the novel coronavirus originated in China. Many companies have been forced into bankruptcy or out of business. What is needed for economic recovery now is not subsidies and regulations by the government, but policies which can utilize the "wisdom of the private sector."

For more information, visit en.hr-party.jp

HAPPY SCIENCE ACADEMY JUNIOR AND SENIOR HIGH SCHOOL

Happy Science Academy Junior and Senior High School is a boarding school founded with the goal of educating the future leaders of the world who can have a big vision, persevere, and take on new challenges.

Currently, there are two campuses in Japan; the Nasu Main Campus in Tochigi Prefecture, founded in 2010, and the Kansai Campus in Shiga Prefecture, founded in 2013.

Nasu Main Campus

Kansai Campus

 **HAPPY SCIENCE UNIVERSITY**

THE FOUNDING SPIRIT AND THE GOAL OF EDUCATION

Based on the founding philosophy of the university, "Exploration of happiness and the creation of a new civilization," education, research and studies will be provided to help students acquire deep understanding grounded in religious belief and advanced expertise with the objectives of producing "great talents of virtue" who can contribute in a broad-ranging way to serve Japan and the international society.

FACULTIES

Faculty of human happiness

Students in this faculty will pursue liberal arts from various perspectives with a multidisciplinary approach, explore and envision an ideal state of human beings and society.

Faculty of successful management

This faculty aims to realize successful management that helps organizations to create value and wealth for society and to contribute to the happiness and the development of management and employees as well as society as a whole.

Faculty of future creation

Students in this faculty study subjects such as political science, journalism, performing arts and artistic expression, and explore and present new political and cultural models based on truth, goodness and beauty.

Faculty of future industry

This faculty aims to nurture engineers who can resolve various issues facing modern civilization from a technological standpoint and contribute to the creation of new industries of the future.

ABOUT IRH PRESS USA

IRH Press USA Inc. was founded in 2013 as an affiliated firm of IRH Press Co., Ltd. Based in New York, the press publishes books in various categories including spirituality, religion, and self-improvement and publishes books by Ryuho Okawa, the author of over 100 million books sold worldwide. For more information, visit okawabooks.com.

Follow us on:

f Facebook: Okawa Books   Instagram: OkawaBooks

▶ Youtube: Okawa Books   Twitter: Okawa Books

P Pinterest: Okawa Books   g Goodreads: Ryuho Okawa

——— **NEWSLETTER** ———

To receive book related news, promotions and events, please subscribe to our newsletter below.

∂ eepurl.com/bsMeJj

——— **AUDIO / VISUAL MEDIA** ———

YOUTUBE

PODCAST

Introduction of Ryuho Okawa's titles; topics ranging from self-help, current affairs, spirituality, religion, and the universe.

BOOKS BY RYUHO OKAWA

RYUHO OKAWA'S LAWS SERIES

The Laws Series is an annual volume of books that are comprised of Ryuho Okawa's lectures that function as universal guidance to all people. They are of various topics that were given in accordance with the changes that each year brings. *The Laws of the Sun*, the first publication of the laws series, ranked in the annual best-selling list in Japan in 1994. Since, the laws series' titles have ranked in the annual best-selling list every year for more than two decades, setting socio-cultural trends in Japan and around the world.

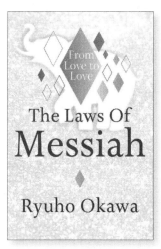

The 28th Laws Series

The Laws Of Messiah

From Love to Love

Paperback • 248 pages • $16.95
ISBN: 978-1-942125-90-7 (Jan. 31, 2022)

"What is Messiah?" This book carries an important message of love and guidance to people living now from the Modern-Day Messiah or the Modern-Day Savior. It also reveals the secret of Shambhala, the spiritual center of Earth, as well as the truth that this spiritual center is currently in danger of perishing and what we can do to protect this sacred place.

Love your Lord God. Know that those who don't know love don't know God. Discover the true love of God and the ideal practice of faith. This book teaches the most important element we must not lose sight of as we go through our soul training on this planet Earth.

For a complete list of books, visit **okawabooks.com**

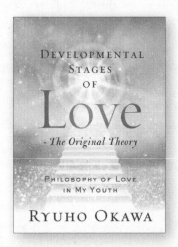

Scheduled to be published in June 2022.

Developmental Stages of Love - The Original Theory

Philosophy of Love in My Youth

Hardcover • 160 pages • $17.95
ISBN: 978-1-942125-94-5

This book is about author Ryuho Okawa's original philosophy of love which serves as the foundation of love in the chapter three of *The Laws of the Sun*. It consists of series of short essays authored during his age of 25 through 28 while he was working as a young promising business elite at an international trading company after attaining the Great Enlightenment in 1981. This revolutionary philosophy, developmental states of love, is the idea to unite love and enlightenment, West and East, and bridges Christianity and Buddhism. It is also the starting point of the global utopian movement, Happy Science.

*For a complete list of books, visit **okawabooks.com***

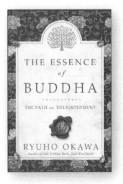

THE ESSENCE OF BUDDHA

THE PATH TO ENLIGHTENMENT

Paperback • 208 pages • $14.95
ISBN: 978-1-942125-06-8 (Oct. 1, 2016)

The essence of Shakyamuni Buddha's original teachings of the mind are explained in simple language: how to attain inner happiness, the wisdom to conquer ego, and the path to enlightenment for people in the contemporary era. It is a way of life that anyone can practice to achieve lifelong self-growth

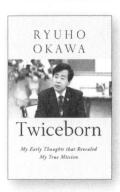

TWICEBORN

MY EARLY THOUGHTS THAT REVEALED
MY TRUE MISSION

Hardcover • 206 pages • $19.95
ISBN: 978-1-942125-74-7 (Oct. 7, 2020)

The incredible story of how Ryuho Okawa achieved enlightenment to become a Living Buddha and Modern-Day Savior. This book is shimmering with inspiring perspectives to improve your life. It is recommended to watch the live action film *Twiceborn* alongside it.

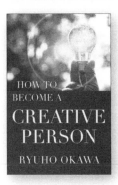

HOW TO BECOME
A CREATIVE PERSON

Paperback • 176 pages • $16.95
ISBN: 978-1-942125-84-6 (Oct. 15, 2021)

How can we become creative when we feel we are not naturally creative? This book provides easy to follow universal and hands-on-rules to become a creative person in work and life. These methods of becoming creative are certain to bring you success in work and life. Discover the secret ingredient for becoming truly creative.

*For a complete list of books, visit **okawabooks.com***

THE TRILOGY

The first three volumes of the Laws Series, *The Laws of the Sun*, *The Golden Laws*, and *The Nine Dimensions* make a trilogy that completes the basic framework of the teachings of God's Truths. *The Laws of the Sun* discusses the structure of God's Laws, *The Golden Laws* expounds on the doctrine of time, and *The Nine Dimensions* reveals the nature of space.

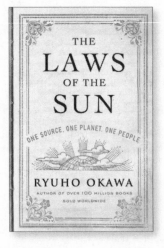

THE LAWS OF THE SUN

One Source, One Planet,
One People

Paperback • 288 pages • $15.95
ISBN: 978-1-942125-43-3 (Oct. 15, 2018)

IMAGINE IF YOU COULD ASK GOD why He created this world and what spiritual Laws He used to shape us—and everything around us. If we could understand His designs and intentions, we could discover what our goals in life should be and whether our actions move us closer to those goals or farther away.

At a young age, a spiritual calling prompted Ryuho Okawa to outline what he innately understood to be universal truths for all humankind. In *The Laws of the Sun*, Okawa outlines these Laws of the universe and provides a road map for living one's life with greater purpose and meaning.

In this powerful book, Ryuho Okawa reveals the transcendent nature of consciousness and the secrets of our multidimensional universe and our place in it. By understanding the different stages of love and following the Buddhist Eightfold Path, he believes we can speed up our eternal process of development. *The Laws of the Sun* shows the way to realize true happiness—a happiness that continues from this world through the other.

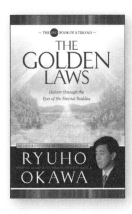

THE GOLDEN LAWS

History through the Eyes of
the Eternal Buddha

Paperback • 204 pages • $14.95
ISBN: 978-1-941779-81-1 (Jul. 1, 2011)

Throughout history, Great Guiding Spirits have been present on Earth in both the East and the West at crucial points in human history to further our spiritual development. *The Golden Laws* reveals how Divine Plan has been unfolding on Earth, and outlines 5,000 years of the secret history of humankind. Once we understand the true course of history, through past, present and into the future, we cannot help but become aware of the significance of our spiritual mission in the present age.

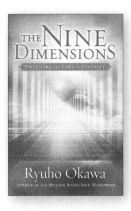

THE NINE DIMENSIONS

Unveiling the Laws of Eternity

Paperback • 168 pages • $15.95
ISBN: 978-0-982698-56-3 (Feb. 16, 2012)

Where do we come from and where do we go after death? Ryuho Okawa provides in-depth explanations about the multi-dimensional universe. The afterlife (spirit world) or multi-dimensional universe, is an orderly place built upon the law of same wavelengths or vibrations and the level of enlightenment.

---

*For a complete list of books, visit **okawabooks.com***

THE LAWS OF HAPPINESS

LOVE, WISDOM, SELF-REFLECTION AND PROGRESS

Paperback • 264 pages • $16.95
ISBN: 978-1-942125-70-9 (Aug. 28, 2020)

Happiness is not found outside us; it is found within us. It is in how we think, how we look at our lives, and how we devote our hearts to the work we do. Discover how the Fourfold Path of Love, Wisdom, Self-reflection and Progress creates a life of sustainable happiness.

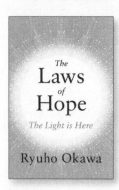

THE LAWS OF HOPE

THE LIGHT IS HERE

Paperback • 224 pages • $16.95
ISBN:978-1-942125-76-1 (Jan. 15, 2021)

Learn the authentic way to realize your hopes based on the Laws of Mind. We attract what is sympathetic to our mindset. Learn the wisdom to conquer life's problems and fulfill your mission of Light. Discover how you can be the hope for the world and the future!

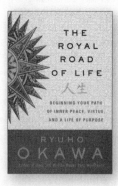

THE ROYAL ROAD OF LIFE

BEGINNING YOUR PATH OF INNER PEACE, VIRTUE, AND A LIFE OF PURPOSE

Paperback • 224 pages • $16.95
ISBN: 978-1-942125-53-2 (Jan. 15, 2020)

What is the essence of a virtuous leader? How do we live deeply and with noble purpose? This book introduces a way of life based on understanding the nature of our mind and gaining mastery over it. It is a guide to maintaining peace of mind and cultivating virtue throughout our life.

*For a complete list of books, visit **okawabooks.com***

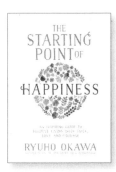

THE STARTING POINT OF HAPPINESS

AN INSPIRING GUIDE TO POSITIVE LIVING WITH FAITH, LOVE, AND COURAGE

Hardcover • 224 pages • $16.95
ISBN: 978-1-942125-26-6 (Nov. 7, 2017)

This self-renewing guide empowers everyone to find strength amidst difficult circumstances and to savor the joy of giving love to others in accordance with the will of the great universe. The book will awaken us to spiritual truths that invite authentic and lasting happiness.

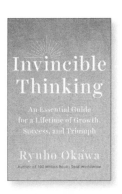

INVINCIBLE THINKING

AN ESSENTIAL GUIDE FOR A LIFETIME OF GROWTH, SUCCESS, AND TRIUMPH

Hardcover • 208 pages • $16.95
ISBN: 978-1-942125-25-9 (Sep. 5, 2017)

There is no defeat in life! "Invincible Thinking" is a dynamite or mighty drill that bores through the solid rock of challenges and difficulties in life. A mindset of invincibility is the most powerful tool to transform any negative karma or circumstance into wisdom for the growth of our soul.

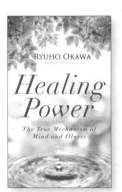

HEALING POWER

THE TRUE MECHANISM OF MIND AND ILLNESS

Paperback • 189 pages • $14.95
ISBN: 978-1-941779-96-5 (Feb. 18, 2016)

This book clearly describes the relationship between the mind and illness, and provides you with hints to restore your mental and physical health. Cancer, heart disease, allergy, skin disease, dementia, psychiatric disorder, atopy... Many miracles of healing are happening!

---

*For a complete list of books, visit **okawabooks.com***

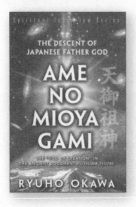

THE DESCENT OF JAPANESE FATHER GOD AME-NO-MIOYA-GAMI

The God of Creation in the Ancient Document *Hotsuma Tsutae*

Paperback • 276 pages • $14.95
ISBN: 978-1-943928-29-3 (Feb. 12, 2022)

By reading this book, you can find the origin of bushido (samurai spirit) and understand how the ancient Japanese civilization influenced other countries. Now that the world is in confusion, Japan is expected to awaken to its true origin and courageously rise to bring justice to the world.

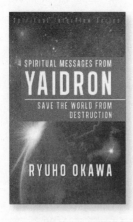

SPIRITUAL MESSAGES FROM YAIDRON

Save the World from Destruction

Paperback • 190 pages • $11.95
ISBN: 978-1-943928-23-1 (Dec. 25, 2021)

In this book, Yaidron explains what was going on behind the military coup in Myanmar and Taliban's control over Afghanistan. He also warns of the imminent danger approaching Taiwan. According to what he observes from the universe, World War III has already begun on Earth. What is now going on is a battle between democratic values and the communist one-party control. How to overcome this battle and create peace on Earth depends on the faith and righteous actions of each one of us.

For a complete list of books, visit ***okawabooks.com***

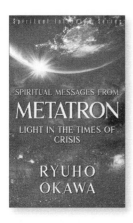

SPIRITUAL MESSAGES FROM METATRON

Light in the Times of Crisis

Paperback • 146 pages • $11.95
ISBN: 978-1-943928-19-4 (Nov. 4, 2021)

Metatron is one of the highest-ranking angels (seraphim) in Judaism and Christianity, and also one of the saviors of universe who has guided the civilizations of many planets including Earth, under the guidance of Lord God. Such savior has sent a message upon seeing the crisis of Earth. You will also learn about the truth behind the coronavirus pandemic, the unimaginable extent of China's desire, the danger of appeasement policy toward China, and the secret of Metatron.

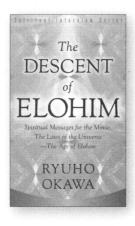

THE DESCENT OF ELOHIM

Spiritual Messages for the Movie,
The Laws of the Universe-The Age of Elohim

Paperback • 160 pages • $11.95
ISBN: 978-1-943928-17-0 (Oct. 12, 2021)

This book contains the spiritual messages from Elohim, the Lord who appears in the Old Testament and who actually led His people about 150 million years ago. Through this book and the movie, The Laws of the Universe - The Age of Elohim, you can learn how life on Earth was like at that time, and how diverse people, who had come from other planets, fought each other until they finally found peace and harmony under Lord Elohim.

---

*For a complete list of books, visit **okawabooks.com***

THE LAWS OF SECRET
Awaken to This New World and Change Your Life

THE TRUE EIGHTFOLD PATH
Guideposts for Self-innovation

THE POWER OF BASICS
Introduction to Modern Zen Life of Calm, Spirituality and Success

THE STRONG MIND
The Art of Building the Inner Strength
to Overcome Life's Difficulties

THE MOMENT OF TRUTH
Become a Living Angel Today

THE REAL EXORCIST
Attain Wisdom to Conquer Evil

THE MIRACLE OF MEDITATION
Opening Your Life to Peace, Joy and the Power Within

THE CHALLENGE OF THE MIND
An Essential Guide to Buddha's Teachings:
Zen, Karma, and Enlightenment

THE LAWS OF FAITH
One World Beyond Differences

MUSIC BY RYUHO OKAWA

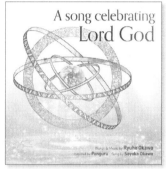
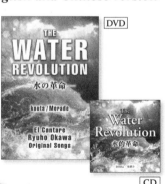